LOBSTER RIDDLES AND RECIPES

LOBSTER LORE, FUN FACTS, RIDDLES, QUIZZES
AND RECIPES

LOBSTER RIDDLES AND RECIPES

J.P. CROSS SCMC

PALMETTO
PUBLISHING
Charleston, SC
www.PalmettoPublishing.com

Hardcover ISBN: 9798822967335

Paperback ISBN : 9798822967342

INTRODUCTION

This is a collection of lobster riddles and recipes created, compiled, adapted and tested by the author over years of travel and experimentation. The goal is to inspire another generation of lobster lovers to enjoy protecting, cooking, eating and appreciating these magical crustaceans. The title of the book pays homage to the fishermen and purveyors of fresh lobsters in Rockport, Massachusetts where the Crosses have vacationed every summer for over a decade. For J.P. and his wife Kim, Roy Moore's lobster shack on Bearskin Skin Neck serves the best fresh lobsters on the planet. Caught daily, they are boiled in briney sea water and served with warm drawn butter and lemon. The 1 ¼ to 1 ½ pounders are the sweetest.

In addition to the classic New England boiled lobster dinner, this book includes a collection of lobster recipes, at varying degrees of difficulty, for appetizers, soups, salads, pastas and main dishes. It may be the most complete collection and eccletic mix of lobster recipes available.

The book also weaves in lobster riddles with the recipes, fun facts, quotes and a lobster quiz at the end to test your knowledge of lobsters.

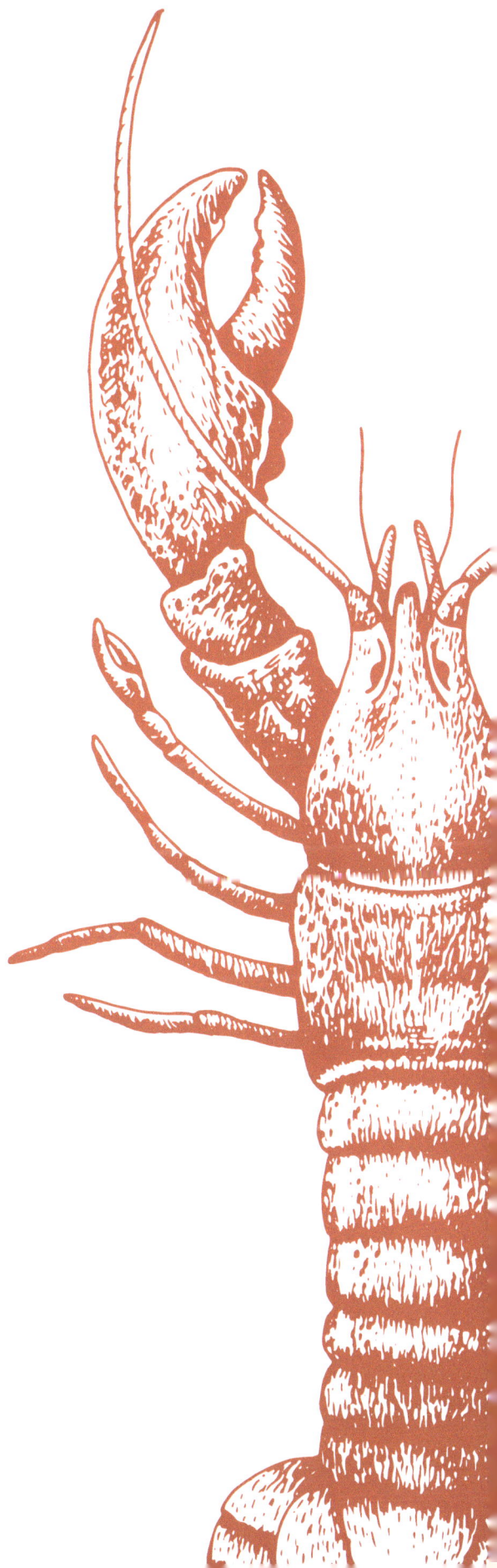

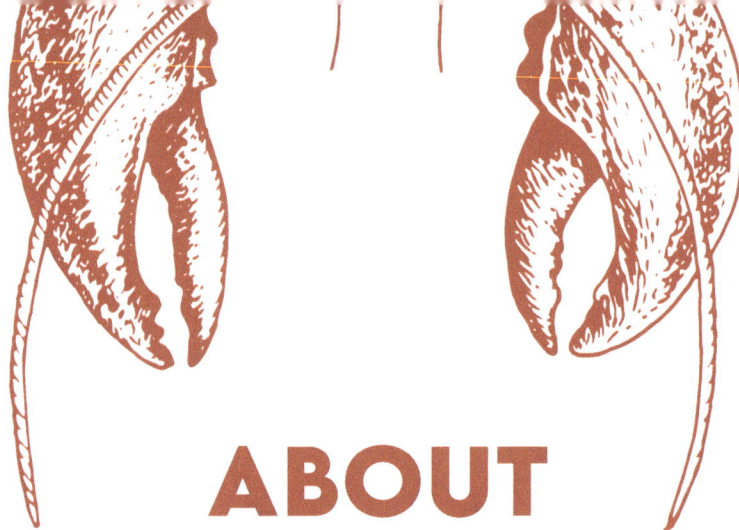

ABOUT
THE AUTHOR

J.P. Cross is a retired professor and international educator. He now spends his time writing, cooking, sailing, traveling, foraging and tending his vegetable, herb and flower gardens in New Haven, Vermont with his wife Kim. Over the past six decades Cross has lived, worked, traveled and eaten his way through 72 countries around the world in North America, South America, Eastern and Western Europe, Asia, Africa, Australia and New Zealand. During the pandemic, Cross challenged himself to perfect selected recipes – mostly seafood - from many of these countries to be taste tested and ranked on a scale of 1-5 by family and friends. After reaching a ranking of 5 on the selected recipes his wife Kim awarded him with a chef's apron that she made and embroidered with the letters JPCSCMC (Self Certified Master Chef).

J.P.'s love of lobster began at a very early age. As family lore has it, he had his first lobster at the age of four or five during a family summer vacation to coastal Maine in the early 1960s. The family had gone to a seafood restaurant and J.P. had his first taste of a freshly boiled lobster from the lobster pound served with drawn warm butter, lemon and a freshly steamed ear of corn on the cob. It was love at first bite. Up early the next morning he and his brother were eager to have breakfast and go to the beach so their parents sent them down to the hotel dining room to have breakfast. Soon after the boys had left, their parents got a call from the dining room to let them know that J.P. had ordered a whole lobster for breakfast....The rest is history.

J.P. Cross in Rockport MA

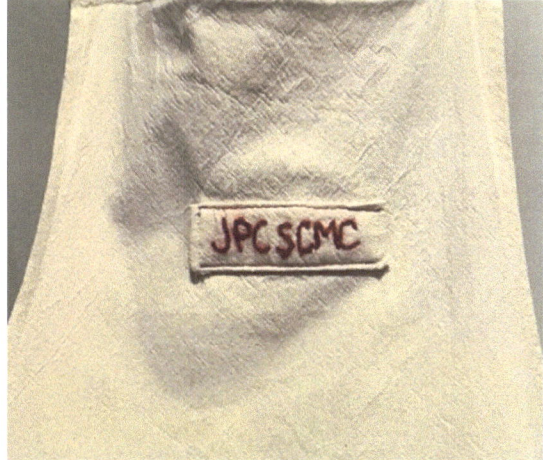
The "JPC Self-Certified Master Chef Apron"

"Some say that lobsters are the cockroaches of the sea. Apparently Marie Antoinette even fainted out of horror when she first saw a lobster. But I disagree. I would never choose to eat a cockroach".

J.P. Cross

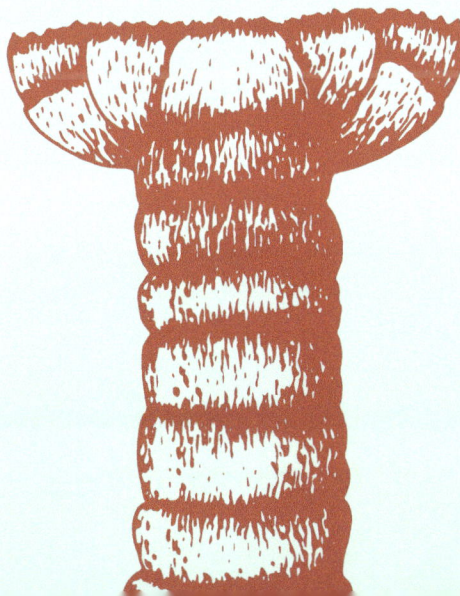

CONTENTS

LOBSTERS FROM INDIGENOUS PEOPLES TO THE PRESENT

JPC'S TOP LOBSTER RECIPES

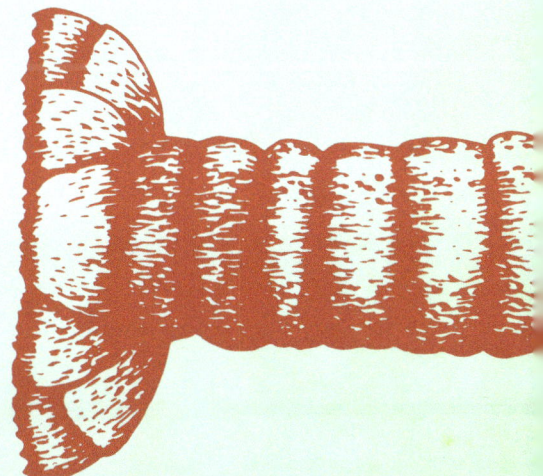

"Europe's the Mayonnaise, but America supplies the good old lobster."

D.H. Lawrence

LOBSTERS FROM INDIGENOUS PEOPLES TO THE PRESENT

WHAT'S A LOBSTER?

Lobsters are crustaceans, which means they are related to shrimps and crabs. More specifically, they belong to the *Nephropidae* family, which includes several different species of lobster.

Among the best known are the American and European lobsters, *Homarus americanus* and *Homarus gammarus* respectively – these are the two species that are most commonly caught for human consumption on either side of the Atlantic.

Lobsters have five pairs of legs – the back four are used for walking while the front two are enlarged, bearing the distinctive claws. Lobsters also have smaller claws at the end of all their walking legs apart from the back pair.

They also have an exoskeleton and a carapace that is shed many times throughout their lives as they grow.

Another important feature of lobsters is their antennae. Since they usually inhabit dark or murky areas of the seafloor, these are important for tasting and smelling the sea around them, which helps them find food.

AND WHAT'S NOT A LOBSTER?

As well as true lobsters, there are also several other species that are often referred to as lobsters – but that are, in fact, not closely related species at all.

One of the best-known of these is the spiny lobster, another type of crustacean belonging to the *Palinuridae* family. Superficially, they look very similar to true lobsters, but there are also quite a few differences.

While they have a hard carapace and exoskeleton like true lobsters, they have much longer antennae, and they also don't have claws on their walking legs – although females of most species have a small pair of claws on their front legs.

Although these animals are only very distant cousins of true lobsters, they live very similar lives and eat a similar diet. Furthermore, most people think of them as lobsters – or indeed aren't aware that they aren't lobsters – so we'll say a bit about the diet of these animals too.

WHAT DO AMERICAN AND EUROPEAN LOBSTERS EAT?

Although there are several species of lobster, we'll stick to talking about the diets of the American lobster and the European lobster – but other species also tend to consume similar diets, depending on their habitat and size. So, what do lobsters eat? American and European lobsters are both omnivorous, meaning they are happy to eat both meat and vegetation. They are opportunistic, unfussy feeders, taking anything that comes their way. They detect their food by using their antennae.

Both species of lobster actively hunts for live prey, but they are also capable of scavenging and making do with anything they find when food is scarce. Here are some common food items for American and European lobsters:

- **Echinoderms**
  One of the favorite foods of lobsters is **echinoderms**, which is a group of animals that includes **sea urchins**, **starfish** and **sea cucumbers**.

- **Polychaetes**
  Polychaetes are a group of worm-like creatures that usually live in the sea – and to lobsters, they are seen as a tasty snack.

- **Other crustaceans**
  Lobsters are crustaceans themselves, but they enjoy eating other seagoing members of this group they meet, such as crabs and shrimp.

- **Plant material**
  When they can't catch live prey or scavenge on dead sea animals, lobsters are also content to turn to plant matter to supplement their diets.

- **Fish**
  If a lobster gets hold of a fish, it will quickly become a nutritious meal. It is estimated that lobsters in Maine now receive around 35–55% of their calories from the herring used in lobster traps there – and after eating, the vast majority then escape to live and feed another day.

- **Clams and other Mollusks**
  American and European lobsters will eat any mollusks like clams and mussels that they come across.

- **Other lobsters**
  Lobsters are cannibals. They are territorial. Big ones will attack and eat smaller ones. I witnessed this firsthand on a lobster boat trip in Rockport, Massachusetts and also heard accounts from lobster fishermen of lobsters fighting in close proximity when trapped.

WHAT DO SPINY LOBSTERS EAT?

Spiny lobsters usually inhabit rocky areas and coral reefs, and like true lobsters, they are also opportunistic feeders that take whatever the ocean brings them. Here are some of the food items usually found on a spiny lobster's menu:

- **Snails**
  Snails belong to the group of mollusks known as gastropods. Spiny lobsters don't care what they're called though and will gobble them down without hesitation. Clams are a favorite food for spiny lobsters, but they will also eat any other similar mollusks like mussels that they encounter.

- **Crabs**
  Spiny lobsters seem to really like crabs but won't take on anything too big since crabs can be armed and dangerous.

- **Sea urchins**
  Spiny lobsters don't seem to mind the spiky defense of sea urchins and will eat them whenever they can.

FUN FACTS ABOUT LOBSTERS

Here are some fun facts about lobsters:

1. Lobsters Are Not Red!

Lobsters come in a range of colors, but red is the one color they are not. They are usually dark in color, which helps with camouflage, but almost all lobster shells contain a chemical called astaxanthin, which is naturally orange.

While they are alive, a protein called crustacyanin suppresses the orange color of the astaxanthin – but when they are cooked, the heat breaks down the crustacyanin, which causes the astaxanthin to turn orange, hence the familiar distinctive hue of a cooked animal.

2. Lobsters Can Grow New Legs

If a lobster loses a leg or even a claw, it can grow it back. This is a useful defense mechanism since if a lobster is caught by a leg or a claw, the leg or claw can be shed, allowing the lobster to escape. Lobster fishers often catch one clawed lobsters or lobsters that have one claw that is much smaller than the other. Lobsters missing a claw are called culls.

It doesn't always save them though, as they are more vulnerable to being attacked by bigger fish or other predators until they grow their legs or claws back.

3. Lobsters Have Teeth in Their Stomach

Lobsters don't have teeth on their mouth to bite food or to chew it before they swallow. However, when the food reaches their stomachs, it is then ground up by three hard plates closely resembling teeth – so in a way, we can say that lobsters have teeth in their stomachs!

4. Lobsters Have Blue Blood

Humans and other mammals – along with many other animals – have blood that is red due to iron-rich hemoglobin. However, lobsters have blood that is rich in copper, making it more adapted to transporting oxygen in colder temperatures – and this makes their blood blue.

5. Lobsters Molt as They Grow

The hard shell of a lobster that protects them would also prevent them from growing, which means lobsters need to shed their shells as they get bigger.

Younger lobsters need to shed their shells around 25 times in their first five to seven years of life, but after this, they only need to shed around once a year. Shedding the shell is arduous work for a lobster, and around one in ten dies during the process.

And why do you never find discarded lobster shells when you walk along the seashore? It's because lobsters eat their old shell once it has been shed – as well as anything else they can find – to reincorporate the calcium into its body as it grows the new shell.

6. It's Impossible to Tell the Age of a Lobster

At present, it's impossible to tell the exact age of a lobster – we can look at the size of a lobster and have a good guess, but there's nothing that can tell us accurately how many years any individual has lived.

However, it's thought that lobsters can live as long as 45-50 years in the wild, at which point, they can weigh up to 20kg (45lbs) and measure up to one meter in length (over 3ft). They can possibly live even longer in captivity.

When lobsters reach this kind of age, they stop molting, at which point their exo-skeleton degrades or collapses, eventually causing the animal to die.

7. Female Lobsters Can Carry Live Sperm for Up to Two Years

After mating, a female lobster can carry around the live sperm for up to two years and can then use it to fertilize her eggs whenever she wants.

Incidentally, a small female can also carry around 8,000 eggs – but a larger one can have up to 100,000! (Source: American Tarantula & Animals.)

8. Seven Largest Lobsters Ever Known to have been Captured

(Source: January 11, 2019 by Jennifer Jones)
Lobster is one of the most popular foods in the world and each year nearly $300 million worth of lobster is harvested in the United States. Fortunately, there are rules over which lobsters can be kept for food and which ones need to be released. All the lobsters on this list were much larger than the legal-size limit and released back into the wild. Some of the famous lobsters on the list have names including Larry, Big Dipper, George, Louie and Rocky. The Guinness world record holder weighed in at a whopping forty-four pounds and 6 ounces!

Larry was another large lobster that was saved from being eaten by well-meaning citizens. This lobster from South Florida was 15 pounds (6.8 kilograms) and ended up at the Tin Fish restaurant. Tin Fish chain founder and owner Joe Melluso estimated that Larry was about 105 years old, and the story was featured in the news.

Amir Rossi saw the story and rounded up his friends to work toward releasing Larry. They paid Melluso $300 for Larry and paid to have Larry shipped back to Maine to be released.

7
Larry

Weight: 15 lbs (6.8 kg)
Location: South Florida
Year Captured: 2016
Image Source: Newser

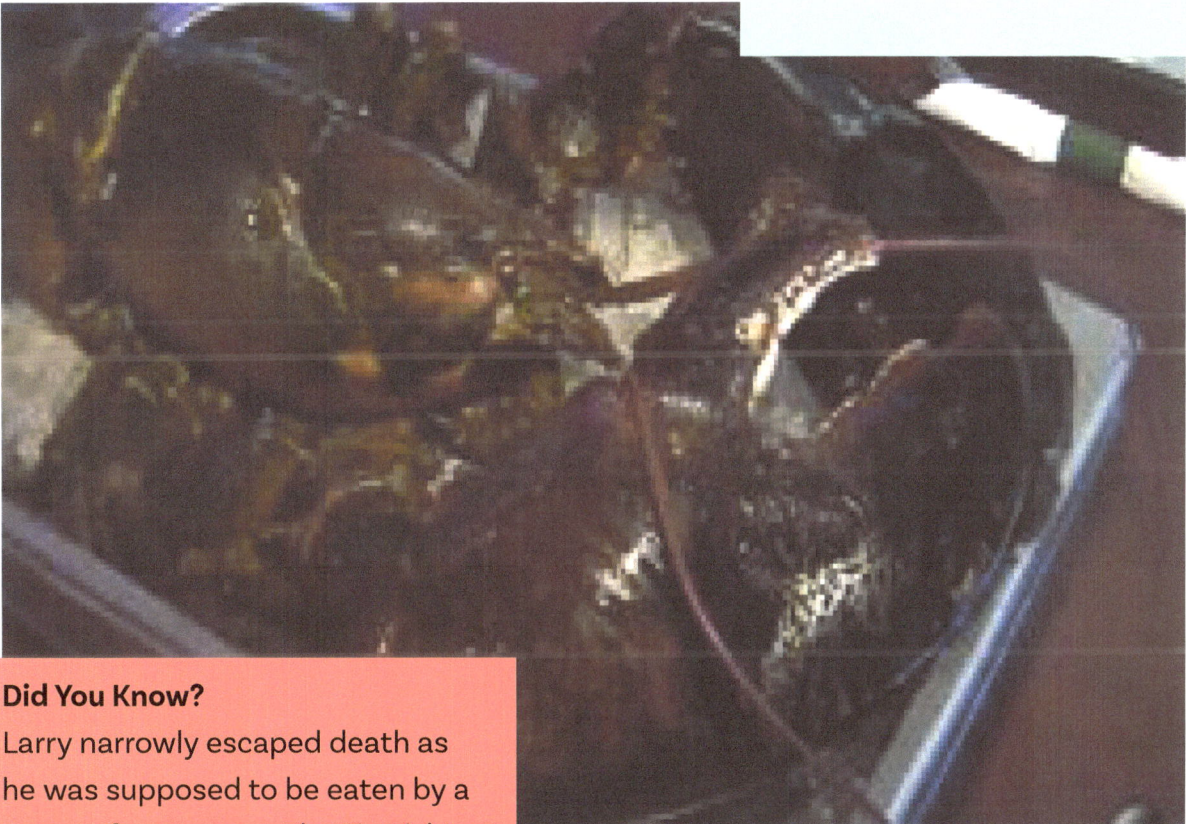

Did You Know?
Larry narrowly escaped death as he was supposed to be eaten by a group of customers. The Tin Fish's Chef Dennis Alvarez offered the customers a 14-pound (6.35 kilograms) fish instead.

In 2015, a photo of a fisherman holding a massive lobster posted to Facebook went viral. The man, Ricky Louis Felice Jr., was working as a deckhand on the Big Dipper, a lobster boat based out of Friendship, Maine. The crew of the Big Dipper said that the lobster was the biggest they had ever seen and estimated that it weighed about 20 pounds (9.07 kilograms).

6

Big Dipper Lobster

Weight: 20 lbs (9.07 kg)
Location: Maine
Year Captured: 2015
Image Source: Pressherald.com

Since the lobster was much larger than Maine's legal limit, the crew had to let the lobster go. Felice and the crew said that they hoped to run across the lobster again someday.

Did You Know?
According to the Big Dipper's captain, Isaac Lash, finding lobsters that exceed the legal-size limit is not actually that rare. Lash said, "I've seen lobsters as big or bigger than that one."

George is one of the most famous lobsters on this list because his story was featured in many international news publications. However, George was featured for his age and not his size, which was only about 20 pounds (9.07 kilograms). According to PETA, who helped get George released, and the City Crab and Seafood restaurant, George was believed to be 140 years old; George may have been the oldest lobster ever captured.

5

George

Weight: 20 lbs (9.07 kg)
Location: caught in Newfoundland, Canada; ended up in New York City restaurant
Year Captured: 2008
Image Source: NBC News

Did You Know?
George was released in a rocky cove in Kennebunkport, Maine, less than a mile from the summer home of former President George H.W. Bush.

George was caught off the coast of Newfoundland, Canada and sold to the City Crab and Seafood restaurant. He lived at the restaurant for 10 days before a customer reported the lobster to PETA, who begged the restaurant to release him. Restaurant manager Keith Valenti said that the restaurant never planned to sell the giant lobster to anyone to eat, but just wanted to drum up some attention.

Unlike the other lobsters on this list, Louie the Lobster wasn't necessarily a lucky find. Instead, Louie had been living in captivity at a restaurant called Peter's Clam Bar in Hempstead, New York for over 20 years. Over the years, Louie had grown to his last known size of 22 pounds (9.98 kilograms)

Butch Yamali, the owner of Peter's Clam Bar, decided to release Louie in 2017 after a customer came in on Father's Day and tried to offer Yamali $1,000 to eat Louie. Yamali decided instead to release Louie and even invited town officials to the ceremony again someday.

4
Louie

Weight: 22 lbs (9.98 kg)
Location: Hempstead, New York, USA
Year Captured: c. 1997
Image Source: New York Post

Did You Know?
Bob Bayer, executive director of the Lobster Institute in Maine assured people that Louie would most likely survive in the wild despite being captive for so long because "There aren't many predators who want to eat a big old lobster like that."

A lobster nicknamed Rocky was caught off the coast of Maine in 2012 and was described as being the same size as a 3 year old child. Rocky was caught in a shrimping net and brought to the Maine State Aquarium. This child-sized lobster weighed 27 pounds (12.25 kilograms) and was over 40 inches (101.6 centimeters).

According to Elaine Jones, education director for the state's Department of Marine Resources, most of Rocky's weight was in his claws, which she said, "would break your arm." Fortunately for Rocky, he was released back into the wild near the aquarium.

3

Rocky

Weight: 27 lbs (12.25 kg)
Location: New Cushing, Maine, USA
Year Captured: 2012
Image Source: Reuters

Did You Know?
Rocky was turned over to the aquarium because Maine fishermen are not allowed to keep lobsters that measure more than 5 inches (1.27 cm) from the eye to the start of the tail.

According to Guinness World Records, the largest lobster caught (officially called the Heaviest Marine Crustacean) was 44 pounds 6 ounces (20.14 kilograms). The lobster was caught off the coast of Nova Scotia, Canada in 1977. Like most of the world's largest lobsters, the Guinness World Record holder was an American/North Atlantic lobster. The Maine Department of Marine Resources estimates that this lobster may have been about 100 years old.

2
Guinness World Record Holder

Weight: 44 lbs 6 oz (20.14 kg)
Location: Nova Scotia, Canada
Year Captured: 1977
Image Source: Guinness World Records

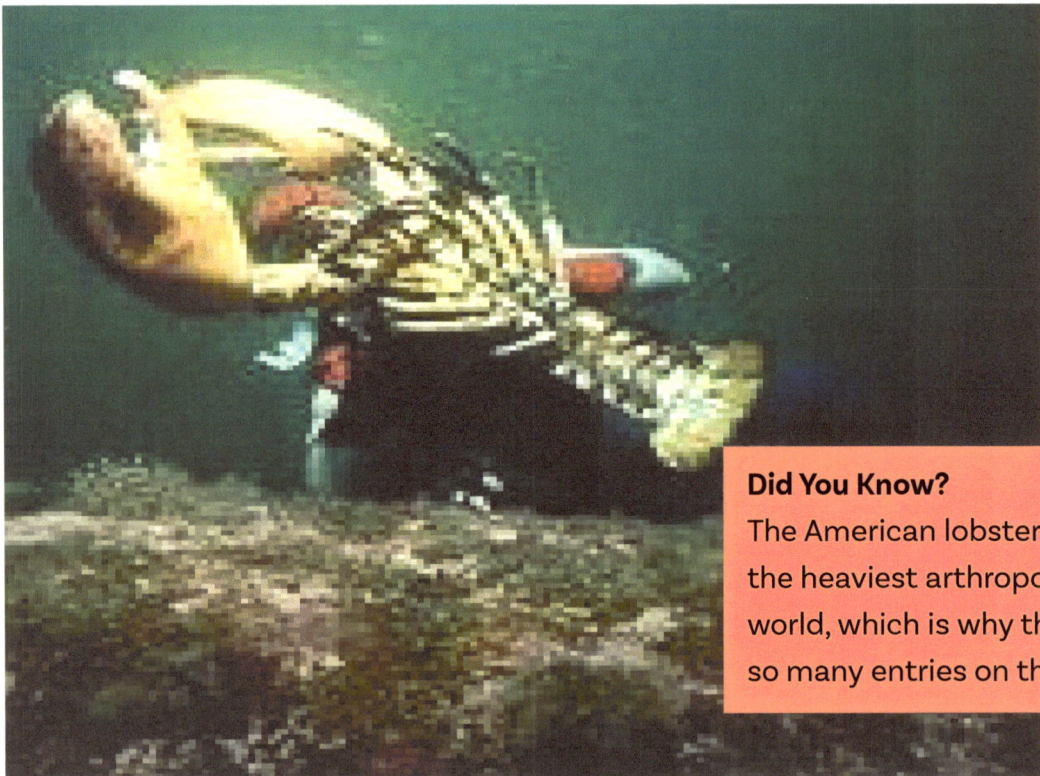

Did You Know?
The American lobster is the heaviest arthropod in the world, which is why there are so many entries on this list!

There isn't much information about this massive 51.5-pound (23.3 kilograms) lobster that was caught in Maine in 1926. The only evidence that it is the largest lobster ever found comes from a picture from a blog discussing some of the world's biggest lobsters. From the photo, it does appear that the lobster was quite large. It was thirty-three inches (83.82 centimeters) in length and its claws were 50.5 inches (128.27 centimeters).

The lobster was also mounted and may have been on its way to the private museum of a man named Charles Q. Eldridge from Mystic, Connecticut. However, the lobster was damaged in transportation and the picture is the only evidence that this large lobster ever existed.

1
Largest Lobster in Maine

Weight: 51.5 lbs (23.36 kg)
Location: Maine, USA
Year Captured: 1926
Image Source: http://www.whoi.edu

LOBSTER FROM MAINE, 1926

Said to be the largest ever caught. Weight, 51½ lbs. Length, nose to tail, 33 in. Spread of claws, 50½ in. After being mounted was smashed in transportation. This picture is the best we can do.

Private Museum of Charles Q. Eldredge, Mystic, Conn.

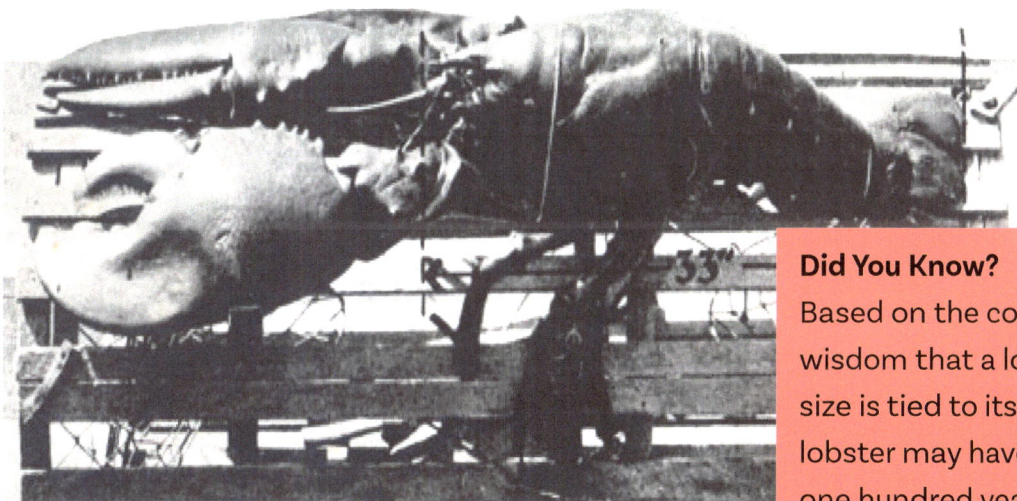

Did You Know?
Based on the conventional wisdom that a lobster's size is tied to its age, this lobster may have been over one hundred years old.

9. The Most Famous Lobster Piece of Art

In 1935 the famous Surrealist Spanish artist Salvador Dali drew an image of a lobster on a telephone. A year later Dali's "Lobster Telephone" was cast as a plaster handset for a telephone and became an iconic example of surrealism, a movement that explored the world of dreams and the unconscious mind. The Surrealist's love of the irrational is captured and embodied in a household object - the telephone from the late 1930s. Here is the picture and the story.

Lobster Telephone was made for the British poet and patron of the arts, Edward James (1907-1984), who was Dali's main patron from 1936 to 1939. Eleven of the plaster lobster receivers were made to fit telephones at James's homes in London and Sussex. Seven of them were painted white and four were painted red.

Salvador Dali's Red Lobster Phone

10. Largest Lobster Sculptures in the World

The World's Largest North American Lobster Sculpture is in New Brunswick, Canada

Shediac, New Brunswick is recognized by locals as "The Lobster Capital of the World" for its lobster fishing industry. In 1989 the Shediac Rotary Club erected a monument as a tribute to the delectable crustacean and promote its role in the development of their community. The late Winston Bronnum from Penobquis, New Brunswick, was commissioned to create this sculpture that attracts visitors and lobster lovers from around the world. The monument stands at 11 m (35 ft.) in length, 5 m (16 ft.) in width and 5 m (16 ft.) in height.

The sculpture weighs around ninety tons; the lobster alone weighs 55 tons while the pedestal weighs around 35 tons. A staircase was erected on the pedestal to allow visitors to climb up on the monument to have their pictures taken.

The Largest Spiny Lobster Sculpture in North America Is Big Betsy in Islamorada, Florida

At 40-feet long and 30-feet tall, Betsy the Lobster, is a giant Spiny Lobster, the type found in the Florida Keys. Big Betsy was modeled after a spiny lobster by sculptor Richard Blaze and is now located at the Rain Barrel artist's village in Islamorada.

Larry the Lobster, the World's Largest Spiny Lobster Sculpture is in Australia.

Australia has a long and storied history of over-sized monuments, and The Big Lobster in Kingston SE, known locally as "Larry", is one of the most impressive. Designed by Paul Kelly and bult in 1979, Larry has kept watch over this small town in South Australia for decades. Larry is a fiberglass-on-steel crustacean standing over 50 feet high and 50 feet long. Paul Kelly from nearby Adelaide, devised the construction of Larry after a local fisherman suggested the idea in order to help promote the area and its seafood.

Guiness World Book of Records Largest "Crustacean" Sculpture in the World is in Hubei, China

Topping the charts though as the largest crustacean sculpture in the world according to the Guiness World Book of Records is in Hubei Province in the Peoples Republic of China. The sculpture measures 18.92 m x 12.81 m x 15.64 m (62 ft 0.88 in x 42 ft 0.33 in x 51 ft 3.75 in) and was built by Hubei ChinaLion Ecological Lobster City Co.,Ltd. in Qianjiang, Hubei, China on 13 June 2015. Lobster is considered a local delicacy.

11. The most famous lobster song:
"Rock Lobster" by the B-52s.

The original 1978 DB Records single version written by Fred Schneider and Ricky Wilson of the B-52s has a duration of 4:37. It has the same lyrics as the re-recorded version, but with more lines during the sequence that lists marine animals. The 1979 single version is edited down from the album version, which lasts about seven minutes and contains an additional verse.

The song was mostly inspired by the 2001 Club in Atlanta, where instead of having a light show, the club projected a slide show with pictures of lobsters on a grill among other things.

The song's lyrics describe a beach party while mentioning both real and imagined marine animals.

I will let you interpret the lyrics but clearly the through line for the song is Rock Lobster.

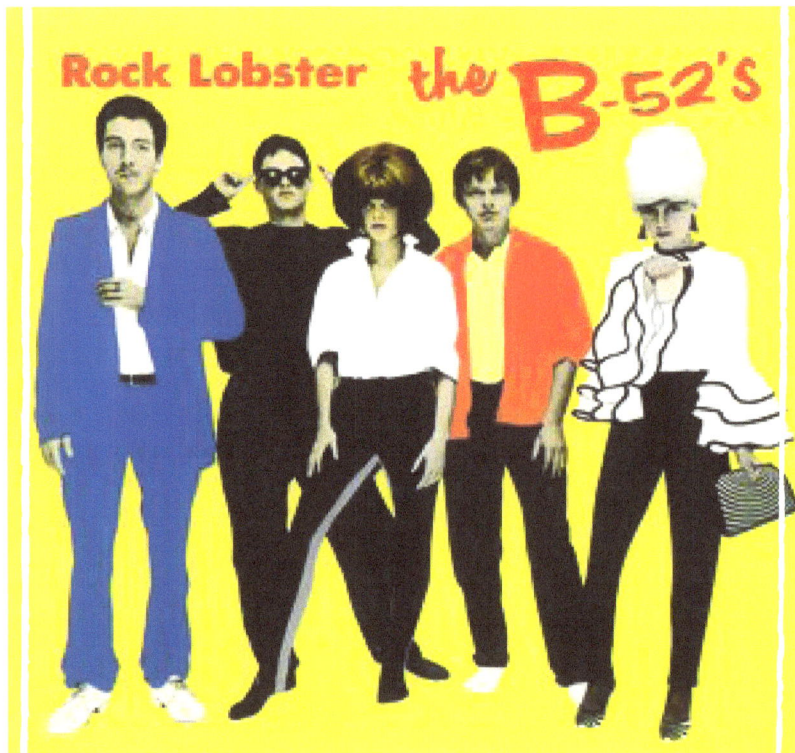

Rock Lobster

Song by **The B-52's**

We were at a party
His ear lobe fell in the deep
Someone reached in and grabbed it
It was a rock lobster
Rock lobster!
Rock lobster!
We were at the beach
Everybody had matching towels
Somebody went under a dock
And there they saw a rock
It wasn't a rock
It was a rock lobster
Rock lobster!
Rock lobster!

Rock lobster
Rock lobster
Motion in the ocean
His air hose broke
Lots of trouble
Lots of bubble
He was in a jam
He's in a giant clam!

Rock, rock
Rock lobster!
Down, down

Underneath the waves
Mermaids wavin'
Wavin' to mermen
Wavin' sea fans
Sea horses sailin'
Dolphins wailin'
Rock lobster!
Rock lobster!

Rock lobster
Rock lobster

Red snappers snappin'
Clam shells clappin'
Muscles flexin'
Flippers flippin'

Rock, rock
Rock lobster
Down, down

Lobster... rock!
Lobster... rock!

Let's rock!

Boys and bikinis
Girls and surfboards
Everybody's rockin'
Everybody's frugin'

Twistin' round the fire, havin' fun
Bakin' potatoes, bakin' in the sun

Put on your noseguard
Hit on the lifeguard
Pass the tanning butter

Here comes a stingray
There goes a manta ray
In walked a jellyfish
There goes a dogfish
Chased by a catfish
In flew a sea robin
Watch out for that piranha
There goes a narwhal
Here comes a bikini whale!

Rock lobster
Rock lobster
Rock lobster
Rock lobster

12. Lobster Reef Sauvignon Blanc

Lobster Reef Sauvignon Blanc wine from Marlborough New Zealand is the only wine label I found that features a lobster on it.

Lobster Reef
MARLBOROUGH
Sauvignon Blanc
WINE OF NEW ZEALAND

According to the label the wine is described as a "refreshing Sauvignon Blanc with gorgeous passionfruit and stone fruit flavors, zips along with firm acidity and finishes long, clean and invigorating." It goes well with lobster and other seafood, seafood pastas, risottos, and salads.

Although the label features a drawing of a North Atlantic lobster, New Zealand hosts four species of "lobsters" none of which has claws like the North Atlantic lobsters. Below are some fun facts about New Zealand "lobsters" published by the New Zealand Rock Lobster Industry Council (RLIC). For more information go to their link below.

https://nzrocklobster.co.nz/lobster-facts/

New Zealand Lobster facts

- The spiny rock lobster (*Jasus edwardsii*; koura) has always been important to Maori (indigenous people of New Zealand) and for much of this century has supported increasingly important commercial and amateur fisheries. Rock lobsters support one of the country's oldest commercial fisheries and are one of the seafood industry's top export earners.
- The commercial fishery has developed through a number of phases as catches have increased in response to export market opportunities. Management of the resource has changed in response to the changing status of the stocks and the expectations of stakeholder groups.
- Since 1990 the rock lobster fishery has been managed within the Quota Management System and governed by a mix of output controls and fishery regulations, including the provision of a minimum legal size, a prohibition against taking berried females and soft-shelled animals, method restrictions, and the requirement that all pots be fitted with escape gaps.
- The current management of the rock lobster fishery is focused on moving stocks to agreed biological reference points and maintaining them at this level or above, primarily through the adjustment of total allowable catches (TACs).

Lobster species in New Zealand

- Lobsters are strictly marine. They all have the same basic body plan, being head, tail, 2 pairs of antennae, no less than 6 pairs of mouthpart appendages and 5 pairs of legs.
- 'Crayfish' or 'Cray' are strictly freshwater and are clawed, i.e., New Zealand's Koura.
- Unfortunately 'Cray' is a common term used for New Zealand's marine lobsters. Koura is the general Maori name for both (freshwater) crayfish and (marine) lobsters.
- New Zealand has four species of rock lobsters (spiny lobsters), the most common of which is the red rock lobster (*Jasus edwardsii*). In Australia this species is known as the southern rock lobster.

Other species found in New Zealand are:

- Packhorse rock lobster/green rock lobster (*Sagmariasus verreauxi*). This lobster is less than 1% of commercial rock lobster landings, and is the world's largest rock lobster
- Deep-water rock lobster (*Projasus parkeri*) is taken occasionally as incidental catch from trawling but is not marketed
- A tropical rock lobster species (*Panulirus sp.*) is found only at the Kermadec Islands.

Packhorse lobster

In contrast the packhorse lobster is green. Its carapace (the protective shell of the head and thorax) has a distinctive shape at the front part and distinctive patterns of spines. The packhorse also has a lack of sculpting on its tail.

As the world's largest rock lobster it has been found to weigh up to 20 kg and reach lengths of 70 cm.

The deepwater rock lobster has a distinctive apricot colour, two prominent rows of spines on its carapace and a central ridge along the top of its tail. It is a much smaller rock lobster reaching lengths of 25 cm.

The tropical rock lobster species is a medium sized species of the Western Pacific. They have a distinctive structure at the base of each feeler that produces a sharp, rasping sound when the feelers move.

Red rock lobster

The red rock lobster is dark red and orange above, paler and yellowish below. The body is spiny, especially on the head. They can weigh up to 8 kg and reach lengths of about 60 cm (excluding the feelers).

13. The Lobster Movie

This 2016 Canne film festival selection portrays a dystopian society where single people must enter into a romantic relationship within a strict time limit of 45 days or be transformed into an animal of their choice. The lead actor, Colin Farrell chooses to be a lobster if he does not find a romantic partner. It is the only movie I know that is named after my favorite crustacean.

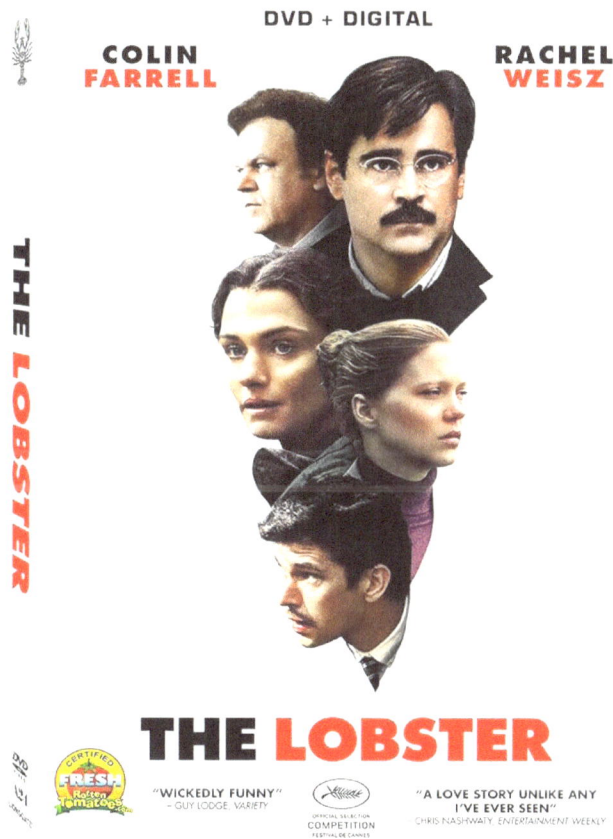

The Lobster Official Trailer #1 (2016) -
Jacqueline Abrahams, Roger Ashton-Griffiths
Movie HD (youtube.com)

HISTORY OF LOBSTERS IN NORTH AMERICA

THE EARLY YEARS

Thousands of years before European settlers arrived on the shores of what is today the Canadian Maritime Provinces and coastal New England, lobsters were a source of food for Native American tribes, most notably members of what is known as the Wabanaki Confederacy. These included most notably the Penobscot and Narragansett tribes. During this early period, lobsters were so plentiful they washed ashore and could be gathered by hand. The Native American tribes ate the lobsters and used their shells as fertilizer for agriculture. They prepared the lobsters by digging a pit in the sand, lining it with stones and then building a wood fire from driftwood collected along the shore. After the fire had burned down and heated the stones they would place layers of seaweed, lobsters, other crustaceans, corn and potatoes over the hot stones. Each layer would be separated by more seaweed. Steaming the ingredients in the salty seaweed and natural juices of the shellfish created a wonderful briny feast. They taught early settlers this same cooking method which is said to have inspired the classic New England clambake.

During the early years of colonization, there were so many lobsters that European settlers considered lobsters to be "poor man's food". They were fed to prisoners and even pigs in New England because it was inexpensive and abundant. There is no evidence that melted butter and lemon wedges were served with lobster during these early years to prisoners.

In the 1860s, when canning food technology developed, inexpensive cooked lobster and other foods were canned to feed soldiers. For the first time Americans who did not live near the shore had a taste of lobster meat. Thus

Photo by Ann Pollard Ranco, a Wabanaki indigenous writer, artist and activist.

began the transformation of lobster from food for prisoners and pigs to a delicacy prized by a growing number of seafood enthusiasts.

Lobster became more accessible and grew in popularity in the early 1900s with the boom in train travel, refrigeration, growing populations and wealth in major cities like Boston, New York and Chicago. Lobster was still relatively inexpensive and was served on trains as a dinner option. Lobster hit its highest prices in the 1920s. This was due to soaring demand which led to unregulated overfishing. Overfishing led to a reduction of supply as lobster populations were decimated. This in turn led to higher prices. The

lobster population did not start recovering until after the stock market crash in 1929 as demand shrank due to high levels of unemployment and reduced available income for many Americans.

On the next page is the 20th Century New York Central System Train menu featuring Lobster Newburg for $2.25. It is the most expensive item on the menu. Based on inflation calculations $2.25 in 1925 would cost $39.44 in 2024. (Source: New York Heritage digital collections)

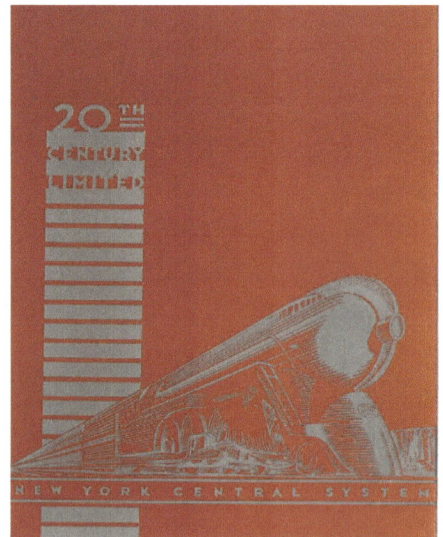

NEW YORK CENTRAL SYSTEM DINING SERVICE

A LA CARTE

SOUPS, JUICES and COCKTAILS

Pot-Au-Feu Fermiere, Cup	.25	Fresh Shrimp Cocktail Lorenzo	.45
Tureen	.35	Clam Bouillon, Hot or Cold	.25
Consomme, Hot, Cup	.30	Clam Juice Cocktail	.25
Jellied Consomme, Cup	.35	Tomato Juice Cocktail	.30
Fresh Fruit Cup	.35	Two-Tone Cocktail	.30
Chilled Prune Juice	.25	Chilled Tomato Juice	.25

Canapes of Anchovy Shrimp .... .65

ENTREES

Oven Baked Beans (Hot or Cold),		Grilled French Sardines, Sliced Tomatoes,	
Brown Bread	.50	Toasted Whole Wheat Bread	.75
Genuine Russian Caviar on Toast	1.00	Broiled Lamb Chops (2), with Potatoes	1.10
Fried or Broiled Spring Chicken (Half),		Roast Prime Ribs of Beef with Potatoes	1.15
with Potatoes	1.10	Imported Frankfurters (Hot or Cold),	
Minute Steak Grilled with Potatoes	1.35	Potato Salad	.70
Small Sirloin Steak with Potatoes	1.75	Eggs- Boiled, Fried or Scrambled	.35
Broiled Ham or Bacon	.70	Poached on Toast	.40
Half Portion	.35	Omelettes Plain	.50
Broiled Ham or Bacon with Eggs	.70	Parsley or Jelly	.65
Fresh Fish, with Potatoes	.90	Chopped Ham or Bacon	.65
		Royal Mushroom Omelette	.65

(Charcoal used exclusively for broiling)

Fried Robbins Island Oysters,	The Famous N.Y.C. Oyster Stew
Cole Slaw, Chili Sauce, Potatoes .65	or Little Neck Clam Stew .65

VEGETABLES

Vegetable Combination with		New Wax Beans in Cream or Fermiere	.35
Poached Egg	.85	Potatoes—Mashed	.20
Carrots and Peas	.25	Julienne, Argentine, O'Brien or	
New Beets Fermiere	.30	Lyonnaise	.25
New Brussels Sprouts with Crumbs	.35	Royal Mushrooms on Toast	.45

DESSERTS

Individual Lemon Cream Pie	.30	Grape Fruit on Ice, Half	.25
Plum Pudding, 20th Century Sauce	.25	Stewed Prunes	.30
French Pancakes with		Preserved Figs with Cream	.35
Orange Marmalade	.35	Apricots, Pears or Pineapple in Syrup	.25
French Vanilla Ice Cream	.25	N.Y.C. Baked Apple with Cream	.25
Hot Chocolate Fudge Sundae	.35		

Orange 15; Sliced 25		Orange Juice, Iced .25
Sliced Bananas with Cream 30	Assorted Cookies 15	Extracted Honey 25
	Orange Marmalade 25	

CHEESE

Liederkranz .... .40	Camembert... .40	Roquefort .... .40

(Toasted Hard or Soft Biscuits served with above Cheese orders)

Cream Cheese with Toasted Rye Bread, Wild Grape Jelly 35

COLD SUGGESTIONS, SALADS, ETC.

Stuffed Olives 35	Ripe or Green Olives 25	French Sardines in Olive Oil 60
Celery Hearts, Iced 30; Stuffed with Roquefort Cheese 50		Sliced Chicken, Tomato Surprise 1.00
Fresh Shrimp Salad 90		Roast Prime Ribs of Beef, Potato Salad 1.15
Sliced Smoked Tongue, Potato Salad 85		Cold Country Ham, Mexican Salad 85
Combination Salad 45 Potato Salad 30	Lettuce 30 Lettuce and Tomato 40	Sliced Tomatoes 30
Pineapple Salad, 20th Century, French Dressing 50		Chicken Salad 90 Chiffonade Salad 35
Mexican Salad 30 Roquefort Dressing 25	Thousand Island Dressing 15	Mayonnaise Dressing 15

BREAD, ETC.

Toast, Dry or Buttered 15	White, Whole Wheat or Rye Bread 15
Cream Toast 45 Milk Toast 30	French Toast with Jelly or Honey 40
Ry-Krisp 15	Crackers 10 Yeast Cake 10

COFFEE, TEA, ETC.

N.Y.C. Special Coffee with Cream (Pot) 25 Coffee (Demi-tasse) 15 Koffee Hag Coffee (Pot for One) 25

Orange Pekoe, India, English Breakfast, Oolong or Green Tea (Pot for One) 25

Postum (Pot for One) 25	Sanka Coffee (Pot for One) 25	Cocoa (Pot for One) 25
Individual Milk 15	Malted Milk (Pot for One) 25	Buttermilk, Bottle 15

Prices are Quoted in United States Currency

Chgo.   B. J. Bohleeder, Manager Dining Service, New York

Enlist in
Our National Defense
Against Infantile Paralysis

Please ask the steward for a coin card to fill with silver, currency or checks. You will find your friends eager to contribute. When the card is filled, send it to the address below. Your money will provide care for the stricken youngster around your corner, and to ward off epidemics of the dread disease.

COMMITTEE for the CELEBRATION of the PRESIDENT'S BIRTHDAY
KEITH MORGAN, Nat'l Chairman
10 East 40th Street, New York, N.Y.

THE 20th CENTURY SALAD BOWL
Ry-Krisp
(Per Person)
60 Cents

For Sales In U. S. A. Only

Martini Cocktail	.40
Manhattan Cocktail	.40
Old Fashioned Cocktail	.50
Creme de Menthe	.50
Apricot Brandy	.50
Medoc	.50
Grand Marnier	.60
Benedictine	.60

Moselle Wine	
½ Bottle, Imported	1.50
American	.60
Rhine Wine	
½ Bottle, Imported	1.30
Sauterne	
½ Bottle, Imported	1.00
American	.60
Claret	
½ Bottle, Imported	1.00
American	.60
Riesling	
½ Bottle, American	.60

Domestic Ale or Beer .30

THE NEW 20th CENTURY DINNER
⊰ $1.75 ⊱

Chilled Celery Hearts

Spiced Pear	Radishes Rosette
Pimiento Olives	Ripe Olives

Pot-Au-Feu Fermiere
Consomme Julienne or en Gelee

Clam Bouillon, Hot	Clam Juice Cocktail
Chilled Tomato Juice	Two-Tone Cocktail
Fresh Fruit Cup	Canape of Anchovy Shrimp

Fresh Shrimp Cocktail Lorenzo

Broiled Lake Trout, Maitre d'Hotel
New Brussels Sprouts with Crumbs, Julienne Potatoes

Poached Eggs Benedict on Peanut Canape
New Beets Fermiere, Argentine Potatoes

Planked Spring Lamb Steak, 20th Century, Carrots and Peas

Broiled Shrewsbury Squab, Guava Jelly, Timbale of Wild Rice
Creamed Wax Beans, O'Brien Potatoes

Roast Prime Ribs of Beef, Au Jus
New Brussels Sprouts Polonaise, Lyonnaise Potatoes

LOBSTER NEWBURG, 20th CENTURY,
New Wax Beans Fermiere, Julienne Potatoes

Served on this dinner $2.25

Romaine, Orange and Avocado, N.Y.C. Dressing

Peanut Muffins   Assorted Rolls   Lemon Raisin Sticks

Individual Lemon Cream Pie Plum Pudding, 20th Century Sauce
French Pancakes with Orange Marmalade
Hot Chocolate Fudge Sundae
N.Y.C. Baked Apple with Cream   Grape Fruit on Ice, Half
or
Cream Cheese with Toasted Rye Bread, Wild Grape Jelly
Roquefort, Camembert or Liederkranz Cheese
with Toasted Biscuits

Tea	Individual Milk	N.Y.C. Special Coffee

Guests will please write on check each item desired.

NATIONAL PEANUT WEEK . . . JANUARY 23rd-31st
NATIONAL PEANUT COUNCIL

Over the past few years even Amtrak has featured lobster in the form of a "lobster crab cake" on its first-class menu.

Lobster Crab Cake.
Photo courtesy of Amtrak

THE GREAT DEPRESSION, WWII AND BEYOND

During the Great Depression lobster demand dropped, the lobster population began to recover, and prices dropped again. By the time of World War II, lobster was once again being canned and used for rations for soldiers.

During these early decades Chefs experimenting with lobster soon realized that Lobster tastes best when cooked live instead of out of a can. After World War II as the economy expanded the demand for lobster began to grow again and prices gradually rose.

Early attempts to farm raise cold water Lobsters were not very successful because lobsters were often aggressive and would attack each other in captivity in confined areas and didn't breed well. Some were even cannibalistic. This is why today, elastic bands are placed on Lobster claws when you see them in tanks at the grocery store or at fish markets. As a result of these unsuccessful aquaculture attempts at raising lobsters, cold water lobsters are still caught in the cold northern waters of the Atlantic Ocean.

As already mentioned, with the expanded consumption of lobster by early European settlers the abundance of the lobsters diminished. They could no longer be gathered on the seashores as the Indigenous peoples had done for centuries in balance with nature. Consequently, the lobster fishing industry was born. In the late 1700's boats known as 'smacks', which had tanks with holes in them that allowed seawater to circulate inside of them, were introduced in Maine to transport live lobsters. It wasn't until the mid-19th century that lobster trapping, which was first practiced in Maine, became the most popular way to collect lobsters. To the right is a 1946 photo of a Maine Lobster Smack and a model 19th century Muscongus Bay Lobster Smack. Muscongus was the name of a Wabanaki village in Maine which meant "Fishing Place" or "Place of Many Large Rocks or Ledges.

TYPES OF LOBSTER

COLD WATER (AMERICAN AND EUROPEAN) AND WARM WATER (SPINY) LOBSTERS

Eventually, Americans also started sourcing less expensive Spiny Lobsters from warmer waters. Typically, Cold Water Lobsters come from the North Atlantic in northern New England and Eastern Canada and Northern Europe. Warm Water or Spiny Lobsters come from Florida, California, the Mediterranean, the Caribbean and South Pacific countries like Australia and New Zealand. The main difference is that while both have five sets of legs and two antennae, Cold Water Lobsters have claws and Warm Water Lobsters do not. Instead of Claws, Warm Water Lobsters have an extra set of antennae for navigation and "whip-like" protection. Without these claws, Warm Water Lobsters are often sold as "tails" because they have hardly any other meat. Multiple factors affect the taste of the meat differently – Such as the temperature of the water, the time of year they are harvested and the anatomy of the Lobster – For example, Cold Water Lobsters with claws can eat some things that Warm Water Lobsters without claws cannot, therefore their diets can differ. Many people say that Cold Water Lobsters are sweeter, perhaps because of the higher percentage of fish and shellfish in their diet. But others really love how Warm Water Lobsters have fuller delicate, tasty meat, perhaps because warm waters might cause faster growth.

Cold Water or Maine Lobster

Spiny or Warm Water Lobster

But whether it's from warm waters or cold, Lobster has become deeply ingrained in the culinary tradition of the United States, Canada, Northern Europe and many other countries around the world.

NUTRITIONAL VALUE, SIZE, AGE AND ANATOMY OF LOBSTERS

Nutritional Value

Though considered a rich and decadent food, lobster meat contains fewer calories than an equal portion of skinless chicken breast. It also boasts healthy omega-3 fatty acids, potassium and the vitamins E, B-12 and B-6.

Lobsters size and age will surprise you.

American lobsters—or Maine lobsters, as they are commonly known—can weigh more than 40 pounds and grow up to 3 feet long. The largest lobster on record was caught off Novia Scotia in 1988. It weighed in at 44 pounds and was 42 inches long. Scientists believe it was at least 100 years old—twice the lifespan of the average lobster. Locals say though the sweetest and most tender lobsters to eat are under 2lbs. A 1 ¼ to a 1 ½ pound lobster is a great size to steam or boil and eat immediately.

Lobsters are known for their unusual anatomy.

Lobster anatomy has changed little over the last 100 million years. Its brain is in its throat, its nervous system in its abdomen, teeth in its stomach and kidneys in its head. It also hears using its legs and tastes with its feet. One of the few features that lobsters have in common with humans is that they tend to favor one front limb, meaning they can be right-clawed or left-clawed. The claw they favor generally is bigger so is easy to identify.

Hard Shell Versus Soft Shell American Lobsters

Hard shell and soft-shell lobsters are different in taste and texture. While both are delicious, and can be cooked and used the same way, I would suggest that hard shell lobster meat is better for recipes that need to have the lobster meat hold its firm texture. Soft shell lobsters are easy to crack, and although the delicately tender and sweet meat can be used for any recipe, I like it best eaten immediately warm with lemon and butter or in a toasted lobster roll (see recipes). Here is a comparison.

	Hard Shell	**Soft Shell**
Yield	Since they haven't shed yet, hard shell lobsters have reached capacity in their shells. The bottom line is that there is more meat and less water in the shell.	Soft shells have recently traded their old, hard shell for a new one with growing room. That extra room in the shell fills with water, making the yield slightly less per pound.
Taste	Hard shells have more meat and tend to weigh more per size than soft shell. Some people prefer hard shell for their firm, dense texture.	Many locals and lobster lovers, myself included prefer a soft-shell lobster. The extra water in their shells while they cook infuses them with a sweet and briny marinade. This tends to make them sweeter and more tender than the hard shell.
Price	Full to the brim with meat, hard shells cost more per pound than their softer counterparts.	Since the yield is a bit less, the cost is less per pound for soft shells. The lower price more than compensates for the extra water weight.
Ease of Cracking	Hard shells can be very tough to get into. Be sure to crack them and have a lobster pick on hand.	Soft shells have a new, thinner shell that is much easier to remove, often with just your hands. Because there is a little more lobster juice be sure to have some paper towels or napkins handy.

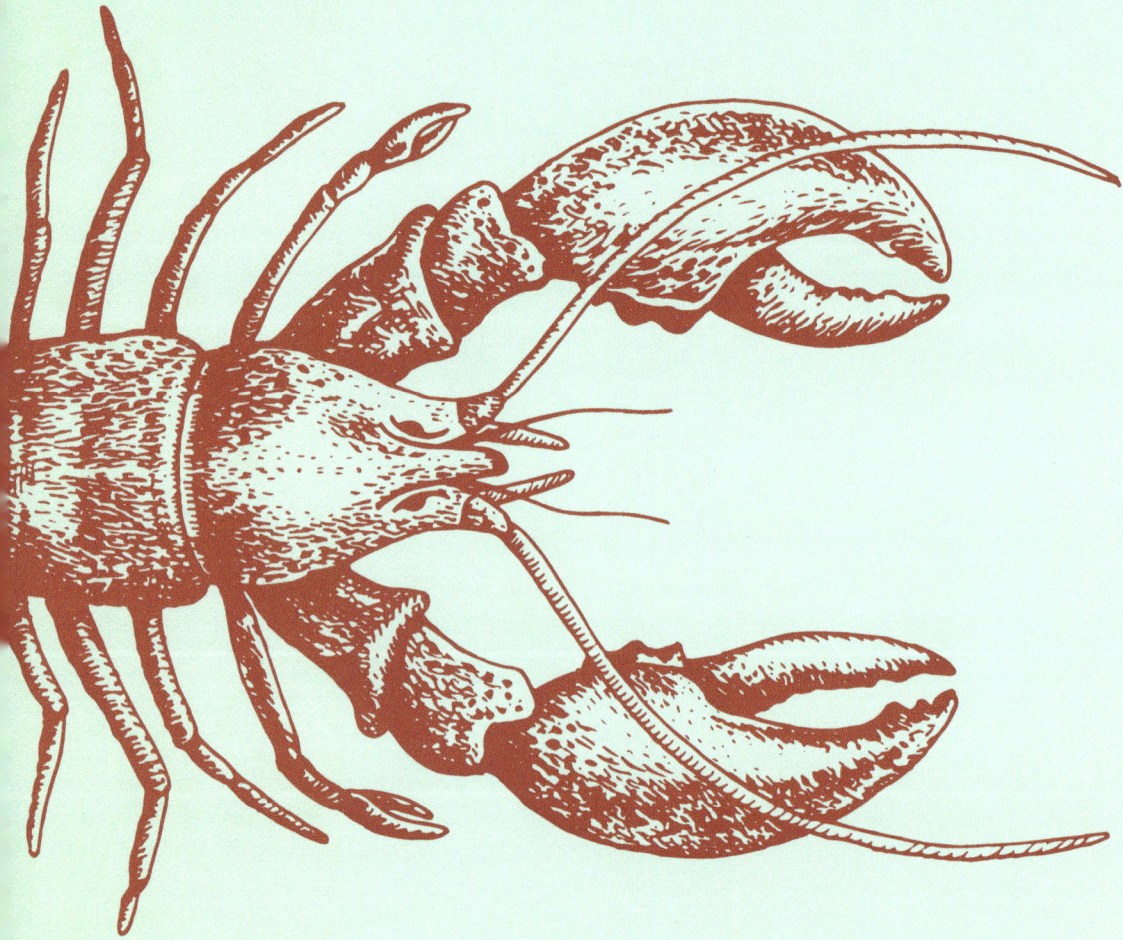

B. JPC'S TOP LOBSTER RECIPES

THE CLASSICS

Lobster Rolls

There are many recipes for lobster rolls from very simple to more complex with multiple ingredients. Below is a selection of my favorites at different levels of difficulty. I have found multiple recipes and names for lobster rolls from Maine to Connecticut and beyond. I even was asked once if I made Vermont lobster rolls. Living in Vermont – a land locked state, I had never heard of a "Vermont lobster roll". That said you can modify a simple lobster roll by adding a little maple syrup to the melted butter and drizzle it over your lobster roll if you want to experiment. Honestly, as much as I love maple syrup, I would not put it on my lobster. Another interesting difference in the recipes I have tried and tasted is the use of mayonnaise or miracle whip. I am a mayonnaise traditionalist but there are those who prefer Miracle Whip salad dressing. You may ask what are the origins and history of miracle whip and mayonnaise and why would some New England lobster shacks use miracle whip instead of mayonnaise in their lobster rolls? Based on a 1952 publication "The History of Miracle Whip" in the Rubenstein Rare Book and Manuscript Library at Duke University, Miracle Whip Salad Dressing was invented by engineers at Kraft and launched in 1933 during the Great Depression. What prompted this new product? Kraft had entered the mayonnaise market in 1926 but sales dropped dramatically during the Depression as penny pinching homemakers starting making their own mayonnaise more cheaply. As a result, Kraft started looking for a new product to develop and market. Their engineers developed a machine to whip the contents for this new condiment so smoothly that the machine was called the "Miracle Whip", hence the name of the new product. The US government Food and Drug Administration has strict standards on what can be call Mayonnaise. Mayonnaise must have 65% vegetable oil by weight. Miracle Whip did not meet these standards so had to be call "salad dressing" as you can see on the label. Back to our question of Miracle Whip versus Mayonnaise in lobster rolls. Kraft rolled out its new product in New England and within eight weeks it was already gaining market share and within six months started expanding to other markets nationally. A new generation of New Englanders were raised on Miracle Whip Salad dressing during the 50s and 60s, including myself. By the 1950s Miracle Whip had 60% of the salad dressing market in the United States. The big difference between Miracle Whip "salad dressing" and real Mayonnaise is that Miracle whip has more sugar and less oil. Kraft marketed the product as lower in fat and fewer in calories than Mayonnaise because there was less oil. They didn't mention the higher sugar content.

Let's turn to Mayonnaise now. Mayonnaise predates Miracle Whip by almost two hundred years based on many accounts. The most told story is that it was invented in 1756 by a French chef during the French siege of the Mediterranean island of Minorca off the coast of Spain. The supposed inventor was the chef of the Duke of Richelieu who was leading the siege. As the story goes, the chef improvised a sauce using oil and eggs because the island did not have any milk or cream. The sauce was a huge success. He named the sauce Mahonnaise after the city of Mahon where the siege and subsequent victory took place. The sauce became very popular in France, and many believe that it was a French invention. Other accounts suggest that the chef learned the recipe from locals who were already making a version of aioli, so was it really a Minorcan or Spanish invention? In fact, I have been told by many of my Spanish friends that mayonnaise is Spanish not French. But then again when I was studying in France, I had a French classmate who insisted that Coca Cola was a French invention.

To summarize, the biggest differences I have found in basic lobster roll recipes around New England are the following:

1. Lobster meat either with or without finely chopped celery.
2. Lobster tossed with Mayonnaise OR Miracle Whip Salad Dressing.
3. Plain lobster meat drizzled with warm butter and a squirt of fresh squeezed lemon.
4. Top sliced buns toasted with either butter or mayonnaise on the outside (I prefer mayonnaise).
5. Plain untoasted buns.
6. Line the bottom of the bun with a leaf of Romaine or Iceberg lettuce or not. (I like the crunch of a leaf of crisp romaine on the bottom. It also helps keep the bun from getting soggy too.)

Riddle: What did Larry the Lobster and his friends do on a warm summer night in Boston?

Answer: They went on a Pub Crawl.

SIMPLE LOBSTER ROLL – A CLASSIC!

(Makes two rolls or double recipe for four)

Ingredients:

- Lobster meat from 1 cooked medium lobster
- 1-2 tbsp of mayonnaise – just enough to coat to lobster meat.
- 1 tbsp fresh squeezed lemon juice
- Salt and pepper to taste. You may add bay seasoning or a drop of hot sauce for taste (your choice)
- 2 hot dog buns
- 1 leaf of iceberg /romaine lettuce per bun

Preparation:

1. Buy the lobster and have it steamed in the store or buy it live and boil at home for 12-14 minutes in salted water until shell turns pink. 1 ¼ to 1 ½ pound fresh lobsters preferred. If boiling at home bring a large pot of salted water to a full boil and place the lobster into to the boiling water headfirst. Once cooked remove the lobster from the water and let the lobster cool.
2. Once cool remove the lobster meat from the shell. Cut the tail and knuckles into bite size pieces. Reserve the claws for garnish.
3. Place the prepared lobster meat in a bowl and add the mayonnaise, lemon juice and seasoning. Mix gently.
4. Open the hot dog buns, place a piece of lettuce on the bottom and fill with the prepared lobster meat. Top with a piece of the lobster claw and serve.

NOTE: You can also just fill the roll with lobster meat and drizzle melted butter over the top instead of tossing the lobster in mayonnaise. I have had it served this way in some lobster shacks in Maine.

LOBSTER ROLL VARIATION #1

Ingredients:
- Ingredients 1-6 above
- ¼ cup finely chopped fresh celery
- 2 tbsps melted butter (not boiled or browned)

Preparation:
1. Follow steps 1-3 above.
2. Add finely chopped celery to the lobster mixture.
3. Melt the butter and gently brush the inside of the buns with melted butter. Be careful not to over saturate the buns with butter otherwise they will be soggy.
4. Place a piece of lettuce on the bottom and fill with the prepared lobster meat. Top with a piece of the lobster claw and serve.

LOBSTER ROLL VARIATION #2

Ingredients:
- Same as variation #1
- 2 tbsps additional butter

Preparation:
1. Same as above except melt butter in a small pan and add prepared lobster meat and seasoning until warm (do not cook)
2. Butter the buns, wrap in foil and warm in a preheated oven at 250 degrees for 10 minutes or until warm.
3. Remove lobster meat from the pan and discard any of the juices or save for another use
4. Add lobster to the mayonnaise and chopped celery mixture
5. Remove warmed buns from the oven. Add lettuce to the buns and fill with the warm lobster mixture and serve

LOBSTER ROLL VARIATION #3

Ingredients:

Same as above

- 2 tbsps cognac
- 2 tbsps mayonnaise

Preparation:

1. Same as above except add cognac instead of butter to the pan and turn heat medium-high. Add lobster and carefully light the pan to flambe the lobster. Let burn for 15-20 seconds and then cover the pan to put out the flame and remove from the heat. Add the celery and butter to the pan and let sit while you prepare the buns.
2. Coat the exterior of the buns with a thin amount of mayonnaise and toast them on a griddle turning once so they are lightly browned on both sides.
3. Remove the lobster and celery from the cognac and butter reduction (reserve for another use – It makes a great sauce if thickened with a little flour or cornstarch). Serve as is or toss the warm lobster and celery with just enough mayonnaise to lightly coat the mixture (optional).
4. Remove buns and prepare the lobster rolls with a leaf of lettuce and the lobster and celery filling.

SMITHSONIAN AMERICAN INDIAN LOBSTER ROLL

Ingredients:

- ½ cup mayonnaise
- 1 tbsp sour cream
- 1 tbsp Dijon mustard
- ½ tsp curry powder
- 1 tsp minced fresh dill
- 2 whole scallions finely chopped
- ¼ cup finely diced tomato
- ¼ cup finely diced celery
- 1-pound cooked lobster meat diced
- ¼ cup chopped radishes
- Cayenne pepper to taste
- 4 hot dog rolls
- ½ bunch watercress, stemmed or other small leave green

Preparation:

1. In a medium bowl, combine the mayonnaise, sour cream, mustard, curry powder, dill scallions, tomato, and celery. Stir to blend. Fold in the lobster, radishes and cayenne.
2. Fill each roll with ¼ of the watercress and ¼ of the lobster mixture.

Riddle: After their pub crawl why didn't Larry and his friends go down any dark alleys?

Answer: They didn't want to get rolled.

There are many ways to cook whole lobsters. The most common methods are to steam, boil or grill them. All these methods are relatively easy. The key is to not overcook the lobsters. Cooking time depends on the size of the lobster and the heat source that is being used to cook the lobsters. **To steam** a lobster, add a couple of inches of salted water to a large pot with a steaming pan placed on the bottom. You can also use a large pasta pot with a strainer. Once the water is boiling, place the lobsters in the pot and cover. Steam for 10-15 minutes depending on the size and quantity you are steaming. **To boil** a lobster, fill a large pot with salted water and bring to a rolling boil. Submerge the lobster headfirst into the boiling water and cook for 10-15 minutes depending on the size and quantity of lobsters. **To grill, broil or pan** roast a lobster, cut the lobster in half down the middle, clean the cavity and follow the recipe. Below are some of my favorite methods and ways to serve whole lobsters.

Riddle: What did Larry the lobster say when he was caught in a lobster trap?

Answer: I'm going to be in hot water now.

STEAMED, BOILED, BROILED OR GRILLED LOBSTER

Method #1

Grocery stores and fish market often can steam live lobsters for you. This is a good method for hard- or soft-shelled lobsters that you are going to use for cold lobster salads, lobster rolls or other hot or cold recipes. You can let the lobsters cool and shell them and use the meat for any purpose. It will keep its flavor and texture in an airtight container in the refrigerator for 1-2 days. My suggestion would be to squeeze a little fresh lemon juice on the lobster meat before refrigerating.

Method #2 American Indian Steamed Lobster

Steamed lobster can also be cooked in a pit as described in the introduction. This is the traditional way native Americans cooked lobsters. To prepare you start by digging a pit in the ground, line it with stones and build a fire over the stones. Once the fire has burned down and the rocks are hot, layer seaweed over the rocks, add lobster, ears of corn with the husks on and potatoes if you want and cover with more seaweed and let steam. Think of this as a classic clam bake only with lobster. You can also add other shellfish to your layers.

Method #3 Boiled Lobster

The best boiled lobster I have ever had is boiled in clear Atlantic Ocean salt water. The next best thing is to add salt to fresh water. Do not use chlorinated or other chemically treated water as it will alter the taste of the lobsters. Fill a large pot that is big enough to hold your lobster(s) with salt water. Bring the water to a rolling boil. When the pot is ready, grasp the lobster by the back and plunge it headfirst into the boiling water. Cover and simmer 7-10 minutes for the first pound, and 2-3 minutes for each additional pound. If there's more than one lobster in the pot increase the cooking time a little. Please note that soft shell lobsters cook faster per pound than hard shell lobsters so adjust your cooking time accordingly. When the lobster is cooked, remove from the pot and place on a solid cutting board. With a meat cleaver crack the shell of the claws, knuckles and tail and plate. A nice trick is to flip the lobster over on its back and with a sharp knife make a clean cut down the middle of the tail. This makes it easier to extract to tail meat. Serve the lobster with a dish of warm lemon butter for dipping, fresh boiled or grilled corn on the cob and any other sides you might like such as boiled parsley potatoes, potato salad or coleslaw. Lobster can be messy to eat. Some restaurants serve plastic bibs with the lobsters. I like to have a bowl of lemon water to clean my fingers and lots of paper napkins.

Method #4 Grilled or Broiled Lobster

I first had grilled lobster in Belgium. It is relatively easy to prepare but requires attention. With this method you can either grill or broil the lobsters. My preference though is to grill them. **The first step** is to prepare your basting sauce. Warm 1 tablespoon of butter and 1 tablespoon of olive oil in a small pan on medium heat until it shimmers but doesn't smoke. Add 2 tablespoons of finely diced fresh garlic and simmer until tender but not brown. Add a ¼ cup dry white wine and reduce by half. Add two tablespoons of chopped fresh parsley, a tablespoon of fresh squeezed lemon juice a dash of hot sauce such as Frank's. This recipe can be doubled or tripled etc. depending on how many lobsters you are preparing. **The second step** is a little messy. On a large cutting board with an edge to hold any liquid, place your live lobster back side down. With a sharp chef's knife cut the lobster in half starting at the head and going straight down to the tail. Remove the inner organs and discard. Rinse and pat the lobster half dry with a paper towel. Sprinkle with salt, cover with plastic wrap and refrigerate meat side up on a plate for 30 minutes. **Third step:** Heat your grill to medium high (approximately 385 degrees). Brush or spray the grill with a high temperature oil such as sunflower or canola oil. **Fourth step:** Remove the lobsters from the refrigerator. Remove the plastic and rinse the dry brine (salt) and pat dry with a paper towel. Place the lobsters shell side down on the heated grill. Brush lobsters generously with the basting sauce reserving some for a second basting and for serving. Close the lid and grill for ~six minutes (depending on the size of the lobster) and then baste again and grill for 4-5 minutes until the shell has turned red and the meat is tender/firm. Do not overcook. Next flip the lobsters and grill face side down for 1-2 minutes to lightly char and provide grill lines. Remove and serve with fresh grilled* or boiled corn on the cob and the remaining warmed butter marinade sauce, fresh lemon wedges and chopped parsley. Season to taste.

*To grill soak the corn, husk on, in water for 2 minutes then drain and place on the grill with the lobster turning each time you baste the lobster.

Riddle: What did Larry the Lobster say when the lobster police took him into the police station for questioning?

Answer: I guess I'm going to get grilled now.

LOBSTER BREAKFASTS

Lobster is very versatile and can be used as the main ingredient, a worthy substitute for other shellfish such a crab or an addition to many seafood breakfasts. Below are some of my time and taste tested favorites.

LOBSTER QUICHE

This is my classic go-to easy lobster quiche recipe. You can experiment with your seasonings depending on your tastes.

Ingredients:

- 2 tbsp sherry (optional but worth it)
- 8 oz. of cooked lobster meat cut, or hand torn into bite size pieces (you can substitute crab, shrimp or use a combination of all three for this recipe which will produce different taste profiles)
- 4 eggs
- 1 cup shredded Swiss cheese or other similar cheese. I have used Cabot Mad River Reserve with great results.
- 1 homemade or good quality frozen pie shell.
- 1 pint heavy whipping cream or half & half

Preparation:

1. Preheat oven to 425 degrees.
2. In a medium bowl with a wire whisk, mix the cream, eggs and sherry until well blended. Add a little seasoning of choice to taste (optional) such as Old Bay Seasoning, Frank's hot sauce, thyme, salt and/or pepper. Be careful not to overdo it with the seasoning since it can overpower the delicate flavor of the lobster.
3. Place the lobster meat and shredded cheese into the pie shell.
4. Pour the cream mixture over the lobster meat and cheese base.
5. Bake uncovered for 15 minutes then turn the over down to 325 and bake for another 35 minutes or until a knife or toothpick inserted into the center comes out clean.
6. Remove from the oven and let the quiche set for 5-8 minutes on a rack before cutting and serving. Garnish with a sprig of fresh parsley and a lemon wedge.

CRUSTLESS LOBSTER QUICHE

This wonderfully delicious cheesy lobster quiche does not require a crust although you can use one if you so desire.

Ingredients:

- 4 oz. grated cheddar cheese
- 4 oz. grated Swiss cheese
- ½ pound lobster meat cut or torn into bite size pieces
- 4 large eggs
- 3 cups milk

- 1 tbsp minced yellow onion.
- ½ tsp Dijon mustard
- 2 tbsps flour
- 1 tsp of seafood seasoning of choice (optional)

Preparation:

1. Preheat the oven to 400 degrees.
2. Spray a large pie plate or similar sized baking dish with oil. I like to use a an 8X11" deep baking dish for this and then cut it into squares to serve.
3. Mix the cheeses together and line the baking dish with the cheeses.
4. Add the prepared lobster meat on top of the layer of cheese.
5. Beat the remaining ingredients together and pour over the lobster and cheese.
6. Bake uncovered for 10 minutes at 400 degrees and then for 35-40 minutes at 350 until the center if firm. Use the toothpick test.
7. Remove from the oven and let sit on a cooling rack for 10 minutes before cutting.
8. Serve with a garnish of fresh parsley and lemon.

LOBSTER BENEDICT WITH ASPARAGUS SPEARS OR SLICED AVOCADO

I had my first and best Lobster Benedict at a wedding in Chicago of all places. It was so good I had to ask the chef for the recipe. Turns out the lobsters had just been flown in that morning from Maine so were still "alive and kicking" but the secret was that instead of using a Hollandaise sauce the chef drizzled the poached eggs and lobster meat with a velvety lobster bisque sauce (see my lobster bisque recipe). The result was a lobster party on my palate. This is a seasonal indulgence that I make during our summer vacations at Rockport. I serve it on a toasted English muffin with either blanched and seasoned asparagus spears or sliced avocado.

Ingredients:

- 4 fresh and high-quality English muffins (no high fructose corn syrup laden cheap imitations for this recipe)
- 1 bunch fresh asparagus, blanched, trimmed & halved at an angle to fit gracefully on the base of your toasted muffin with the heads of the spears just exposed over the edge.
- 8 fresh eggs poached (preferably local free range – freshness makes a difference)
- 4 lobster tails shelled and halved (save the claws and knuckles for a lobster salad, roll, or other use)
- 32 oz. of creamy lobster bisque. (I prefer my homemade bisque, but a high-quality prepared bisque can also work such as Legal Sea Foods Lobster Bisque)
- 2 tbsps fresh parsley finely chopped.

Preparation:

1. Toast the English muffin halves. Lightly butter each half with butter (optional – but butter is better) and place each half in a shallow bowl.

2. Blanch the asparagus and put them in an ice bath for a minute to stop cooking and retain color and firmness. Do not overcook. They should be tender but still firm. Sprinkle with a pinch of finishing salt such as Maldon's. If you are not an asparagus fan you can substitute the asparagus with thin slices of Avocado. I like both options.

3. Carefully placed the poached eggs on top of the asparagus stalks or sliced avocado. Poaching eggs can be a little intimidating but is not that difficult if you follow a few tips. Here they are a) Use the freshest eggs possible, since fresh eggs have the highest ratio of thick white to thin. As eggs age, the whites become thinner, which translates to more wispy bits; b) Cook eggs below a boil at a gentle simmer. If the water is boiling very hard, the whites will form a more irregular shape; c) For more evenly shaped poached eggs, you can strain away the runnier part of the egg white by cracking the egg into a ramekin or small bowl and then gently pouring it through a slotted spoon or fine mesh strainer into a second ramekin to drain away the thin part of the white. Carefully transfer the egg back to the first ramekin for poaching. Or, if using a strainer, slide egg straight from strainer to water; d) To make poached eggs ahead of time, store poached eggs in the fridge in a bowl of cold water for up to 3 days. Warm the eggs back up by transferring to a bowl of warm water before serving.

4. Add half the lobster tail to each muffin half.

5. Ladle ¼ cup of the warmed lobster bisque over the top of each muffin and sprinkle with fresh chopped parsley.

Riddle: Who is Larry the lobster's favorite saint?

Answer: Benedict

APPETIZERS

SIMPLE AND DELICIOUS 5 INGREDIENT LOBSTER RANGOON

As I continue to say, lobster meat is wonderfully versatile because of its texture and flavor and can be used in a variety of appetizer recipes as an upscale replacement for shrimp, surimi or imitation crab. Lobster Rangoon is one of my favorite examples of this. Below are two recipes. The first is a simple classic version and the second add a little more complexity of flavor with ginger, sesame oil and tamari (soy) sauce. For these recipes I am using prepared wonton wrappers that can be found in most good grocery stores and Asian markets. My advice is to check the ingredients. Some are gluten free and very "clean" in terms of ingredients. Others not so much. Alternatively, you can make your own if you have the time.

Ingredients:

- 3 oz. softened cream cheese (I like to use Neufchatel)
- 2 finely chopped green onions (use both white and green parts)
- 1 tsp finely minced garlic (for better flavor mince your own if you can rather than using precut/prepared)
- ¼ cup finely chopped cooked lobster meat
- 16 wonton wrappers (double recipe for 32 etc.

Preparation:

1. In a small bowl beat cream cheese until smooth.
2. Gently stir in green onions, garlic and lobster
3. Prepare a small bowl with water to use to moisten the edges of the wonton wrappers.
4. Place 4 wrappers on a flat dish and with your finger moisten just the edges with water.
5. Place 1-1/2 tsp of the lobster filling in the center of the wrapper. Be careful not to overfill.

6. Fold the opposite corners of the wrapper to make a triangle and gently press all the edges to seal.
7. Place the filled wrappers on a flat baking dish lined with parchment paper so they don't stick.
8. Repeat the process until all the wrappers are filled and ready to fry.
9. In an electric skillet or non-stick frying pan heat 1 inch of a high heat tolerant vegetable oil such and sunflower or canola oil (not olive oil) to 375 degrees. Fry the wontons carefully in batches turning once to make sure that both sides are golden brown. Remove with a slotted spoon and place on paper towel to drain.

You can serve these with a sauce of choice. Personally, I like to use a sweet chili sauce. I add a little more heat though to balance the sweet but not so much as to overpower the lobster filling.

Riddle: Where do lobsters like to go on their honeymoon?

Answer: Rangoon

DRAGON LOBSTER RANGOON

This version is my go-to favorite for entertaining. As with most recipes that require multiple ingredients it is good to do all the prep in advance, so you are not scrambling for ingredients at crunch time.

Ingredients:

- 1 clove garlic minced
- 1 tsp fresh minced ginger
- 1 green onion minced
  (use the whole onion
- 1-1/2 tsp tamari soy sauce

- 4 oz softened cream cheese
- 4 oz chopped fresh lobster meat
- 1 ½ tsp sesame oil
- 1 ½ tsp vegetable oil

Preparation:

1. Heat oil in a pan over medium heat. Add garlic and ginger and cook gently until fragrant but not browned 1-2 minutes.
2. Mix in soy sauce, cream cheese, lobster meat and green onions until well blended. Remove from the heat and place in a separate bowl to cool.
3. Once cooled follow steps 4-9 above noting that this recipe is for 32 wontons.

I serve this with the same sweet – hot chili dipping sauce. I also add fresh cut raw cucumbers and pickled vegetables to the appetizer.

LOBSTER SUPPLI OR ARANCINI

Suppli and Arancini are regional Italian rice balls. Suppli are associated more with Rome and the Lazio region of Italy. The word "suppli" is derived from the French word "surpris" or surprise. Traditional suppli are made with arborio rice (risotto) cooked in a tomato and meat sauce. The risotto is then formed into elongated croquettes wrapped around a piece of mozzarella. The croquettes are then rolled in bread crumbs and fried. The "surprise" is the melted mozzarella in the middle. Arancini or "little oranges" are associated more with Sicily and often include meat and peas as opposed to a tomato sauce. That said both suppli and arancini can be made with any risotto you make. The real difference these days is the shape. Arancini generally are round or conical and larger while suppli are generally more oblong in shape and somewhat smaller. Versions of Suppli and Arancini now appear on menus throughout Italy and in Italian restaurants around the world. Despite the different shapes and sizes, the concept is the same: Prepare a wonderfully flavorful risotto of your choice using Italian arborio rice to make your rice balls. Often, I will make a large risotto for a meal and then use the leftovers for the rice balls. The recipe below is for a lobster risotto and suppli/arancini. Again, you can make this dish with many different ingredients including vegetarian options or meat-based sauces.

Ingredients:

For the stock to cook the risotto (rice)

- 2 1-1/4 to 1-1/2-pound lobsters
- 1 stalk celery roughly chopped
- 1 carrot roughly chopped
- 1 onion roughly chopped
- 3 gloves crushed garlic
- 2 halved and quartered Roma style tomatoes
- 1 fresh hot cayenne pepper (pepperoncino) coarsely chopped

For the Suppli/Arancini

- 1 egg
- 1 cup flour
- 1 cup or more fine panko or bread crumb
- Vegetable oil for frying

For the Risotto

- 1 cup arborio rice (rinsed and drained)
- Strained lobster stalk for liquid
- 2 tbsps butter
- 1 tbsp extra-virgin olive oil
- 2 cloves garlic finely chopped
- 1 yellow onion finely chopped
- 1 can of tomato paste
- 1 crushed dried Calabrian hot pepper (pepperoncino)
- 2 cups dry white wine such as pinot grigio
- ½ cup fresh chopped parley
- 2 tbsps freshly squeezed lemon juice
- 1 tsp saffron
- 2/3 cup freshly grated parmigiano cheese
- 1 cup reserved stock

Preparation for the Risotto

1. Bring a large pot of salted water to a boil. You need a big enough pot to submerge your lobsters. Once boiling, add all the ingredients for the stock in the pot except the lobsters. Bring back to a gently boil and let simmer for five minutes.

2. Next, raise to heat to a rolling boil. Add the lobster headfirst into the stock and cook for 8-10 minutes. You do not want to overcook the lobster as you will cook it more once you make the risotto. Remove the lobsters and let cool enough to handle. Cut the lobster in half, clean the body cavity, crack the claws and knuckles, remove all the meat and set aside. Return the clean body and shells to the stock pot and let simmer for 30-45 minutes. The longer the better to extract the flavor from the lobster shells.

3. Meanwhile in a large deep dish heavy Dutch oven or similar dish melt on low to medium heat the butter and add oil, garlic, onions and pepperoncino. Cook for 1-2 minutes then add the rice and cook stirring for 1-2 minutes on medium heat. Next add the tomato paste and white wine. You can even mix the tomato paste and wine together in advance to save a step. Stir until the wine is reduce and absorbed by the rice.

4. Strain the stock. Reserve the liquid and discard the rest (or use the shells for compost like the native Americans did).

5. Add the stock a ladle at a time as the rice continues to cook. Add the saffron and stir. Keep the rice moist but don't drown it or let it burn. This is the critical stage in making risotto. You cannot walk away and leave it. Gently stir it and add stock as needed until it is tender but firm (Al Dente). The risotto should be creamy by not "saucy".

6. At the end add the lemon juice and stir. Then add the parmigiano cheese and parsley. Serve immediately with additional cheese, parsley and lemon if desired.

If using the risotto or the leftovers for your suppli/arancini, let cool and refrigerate for a few hours or overnight untilled chilled and easy to handle.

Preparation for the Suppli/Arrancini

1. Place three shallow bowls in a preparation line. Place the flour in the first, whisk the egg with a little milk in the second, and place the panko in the third.
2. Heat the oil in a skillet or electric fryer until it is shimmering but not smoking.
3. With a spoon or small ice cream scoop take the risotto from the bowl and form a ball in your hands. Dip the rice ball in the flour, then the egg and then the panko. Place on a sheet pan and repeat the process until you have made all your rice balls.
4. Gently place your rice balls in the simmering oil with a slotted spoon. Do not crowd. Let them sit until they are firm and light brown then turn gently. Cook in batches until completed. Remove and place on a paper towel. Serve plain or with melted lemon and parsley butter, olive oil and herbs, aioli, a lemon and parmigiano béchamel, tomato or other sauce of choice.
5. The suppli/arancini can be reheated in the oven on a cooky sheet at 400 degrees. They can also be prepared in advance and frozen for later use.

LOBSTER RAMEKINS

Ingredients:

- Meat of the equivalent of a 2lb lobster, cooked, shelled and coarsely chopped
- 2 tbsp butter
- 1 shallot, minced
- 4 mushrooms, sliced
- 2 tbsps flower
- 1 cup milk or half and half

- 2 tbsps sherry
- ½ tsp paprika
- A dash of hot sauce such as Frank's
- Buttered bread crumbs
- Freshly grated parmigiano cheese
- Chopped parsley
- Lemon wedges

Preparation:

1. Heat butter in a small pan, add shallot and mushrooms, saute for 2 minutes. Stir in flour and mix well with a whisk
2. Slowly whisk in the milk/cream, add the sherry and cook until thickened. Sir in the lobster meat, paprika and hot sauce and season with salt and pepper if necessary.
3. Divide the mixture int 6 ramekins or scallop shells, top with buttered crumbs and parmigiano. Brown under a preheated broiler until bubbling and golden.
4. Sprinkle with chopped parsley and a lemon wedge to serve.

SOUPS AND SALADS

SOUPS

LOBSTER BISQUE

Ingredients (4 servings)

- Kosher salt
- 2 live lobsters, weighing around 3 pounds total
- 2 tbsps olive oil
- 1 carrot, chopped
- 2 ribs celery, chopped
- 1 medium onion, chopped
- 2 cloves garlic, crushed
- 2 sprigs fresh thyme
- 2 sprigs fresh tarragon
- 2 tbsps tomato paste
- 1 cup medium sherry
- 2 cups fish stock or clam broth
- ½ cup long-grain white rice
- 1 cup heavy cream
- Cayenne pepper, to taste

Preparation:

Step 1: Fill a large pot with ½ inch of water. Stir in 2 teaspoons kosher salt and bring the water to a boil. Add the lobsters, cover with a tight-fitting lid and return the water to a boil. Once boiling, lower the heat to a gentle boil and cook the lobsters until they are bright red, about 12 minutes. Remove the lobsters, reserving the liquid. When the lobsters have cooled slightly, place them in a bowl and remove the meat from the claws and tail, again reserving any liquid that comes out of the shells. Chop the meat and refrigerate. Roughly chop the shells into small pieces and reserve, along with all the lobster remains.

Step 2: Swirl the olive oil in a large pot over medium heat, then add the vegetables and herbs. Sweat until the onions are translucent, about 5 minutes, then increase the heat to medium-high and add the lobster shells and remains. Sauté for 5 to 6 minutes, then add the tomato paste and cook for an additional 3 to 4 minutes.

Step 3: Add the sherry, then ignite or cook until the alcohol has evaporated. Add fish stock and 1 cup of the lobster-cooking liquid. Bring to a simmer and cook, covered, for 1 hour.

Step 4: Strain the broth through a colander, pressing down hard on the solids to extrude as much liquid as possible. Wipe out the pot and pour in the broth. Add the rice and cook for at least 30 minutes, or until the grains are cooked to extreme softness.

Step 5: Blend the bisque in a food processor or blender, then pass through a fine sieve, again pressing down hard on what solids remain. Add the cream and bring to a low simmer. Add the chopped lobster meat, let it heat through, then season to taste with salt and cayenne.

Riddle: What track and field event does Larry the Lobster always win?

Answer: The Bisqueus

LOBSTER AND SWEET CORN SOUP

Along with lobster bisque this one ranks among my favorites!

Ingredients

- 4 1 ¼ pound lobsters
- 4 tbsps butter
- ½ cup fennel finely diced
- ½ cup diced pancetta
- 2 medium leeks, chopped
- 1 cup dry white wine
- ½ cup heavy cream
- 1 jalapeno pepper, seeded and diced
- 4 cups fresh sweet corn
- Freshly ground pepper
- 1 tbsp fresh tarragon copped
- ¼ cup parsley chopped
- ½ cup buttered croutons

Preparation:

1. Fill a large stockpot with 2 inches of water, add 1 teaspoon of salt and bring to a boil. Put the lobster in the water, headfirst, cover and cook for 5 minutes or until they turn red. Remove from the pot to cool and reserve the cooking water.
2. Remove the claws and knuckles and twist off the tail of each lobster. Split the tail lengthwise and remove the meat. Discard the black intestinal vein and cut the meat from the tail, claws and knuckles into bite size pieces (about ½ inch).
3. Return the lobster shells to the liquid in the pot and simmer over medium heat for 20 minutes. Strain into a bowl and let stand for 10 minutes. Pour off and reserve 6 cups of the liquid, leaving behind any grit at the bottom.
4. In a large saucepan, melt 2 tablespoons of butter. Add the pancetta and cook over low heat until browned, about 5 minutes. Add the fennel and cook until wilted. Transfer the fennel and pancetta to a plate.
5. Add the remaining 2 tablespoon of butter to the pan. Stir in the leeks and saute for 5 minutes. Add the wine and reduce over medium heat to 4 minutes.
6. Stir in the reserved lobster stock, cream, jalapeno and season with salt and pepper to taste. Add the corn and simmer until tender – about 10 minutes.
7. Add the fennel, pancetta, lobster meat, tarragon and parley, bring to a low boil to warm thoroughly. Spoon into bowls and top with croutons.

Riddle: Why doesn't Larry the

lobster tell secrets in a corn field?

Answer: Because he is surrounded by ears.

SINGING BEACH LOBSTER STEW

This recipe comes from the Singing Beach in Manchester-By-The Sea in Massachusetts. Singing or whistling sands is a natural sound phenomenon of up to 105 decibels that is reported to occur in over 35 locations around the world including Manchester-By-The Sea, Michigan, Indiana, Nevada, Hawaii as well as Wales, China, Japan, Qatar, Namibia and Egypt. The recipe is simple and delicious.

Ingredients:

- 1 pound raw or slightly cooked lobster meat cut into bite size pieces
- 2 tbsps butter
- 2 tbsps sherry (optional but recommended)
- 1 tbsp flour
- 4 cups milk
- Salt and pepper to taste.
- Lemon wedges

Preparation:

1. Melt butter in a Dutch oven or heavy soup pot.
2. Add lobster meat to the butter and raise the heat until the lobster starts to turn pink but is still tender. Do not overcook.
3. Add sherry to the pot, heat and carefully ignite. Let the sherry cook off for 10 seconds then cover to put out any remaining flame.
4. Remove the lobster and set aside.
5. Lower the heat and add the flour and mix until the flour has formed a paste and is slightly browned. Remove from the heat and whisk in some of the milk. Return to the heat and gradually pour in the rest of the milk whisking constantly until smooth.
6. Add the lobster, heat through and serve with a wedge of lemon.

SALADS

LOBSTER SALAD

This is a classic and simple lobster salad that can be served on a simple bed of Boston (bib) lettuce or used in a more complex green salad with arugula, romaine and/or other greens. It can also be used as the filling for a lobster roll.

Ingredients:

- 8 oz. of lobster meat cut into bite size pieces. Reserve pieces of the claws for garnish if desired.
- 1 tbsp finely diced sweet onions (or more to taste).
- 1 tbsp finely diced celery hearts (or more to taste).
- 1 tbsp freshly squeezed lemon juice.
- ¼ tsp of hot sauce such as Frank's or to taste

- A pinch of seafood seasoning such as Old Bay or to taste.
- 2 tbsps mayonnaise such as Hellman's Real Mayonnaise or alternatively make your own. Good mayonnaise is a key ingredient for this salad, so I do not advise using salad dressing, miracle whip or other substitutes.

NOTE: If you are using a hot sauce and seafood seasoning you may not need to add any additional salt or pepper. Be sure to taste test before adding any additional seasoning. Adjust seasoning according to taste.

Preparation:

1. In a medium size bowl mix the mayonnaise, lemon juice, hot sauce and seasoning until well blended.
2. Add onion and celery and mix gently until coated.
3. Add the lobster meat and mix gently until coated.
4. Serve immediately or chill covered in the refrigerator for up to one hour before serving.

LOBSTER SALAD WITH TARRAGON VINAIGRETTE

This is a very elegant and tasty summer salad. It can be served as a side salad or a main lunch salad. You can easily increase to the ingredients depending on the size or number of servings.

Ingredients:

- 2 1-1/4-1-1/2 pound lobsters
- 2 shallots minced
- 2 tsps chopped fresh tarragon
- 2 tsps chopped fresh parsley
- ¼ tsp salt
- ¼ tsp pepper
- ½ cup extra virgin olive oil
- 3 tbsps freshly squeezed lemon juice.
- 2 tbsps white whin vinegar
- 1 head bib lettuce or romaine
- For the garnish prepare a variety of fresh sweet cherry tomatoes (yellow and red) and slice in half, sprigs of fresh tarragon and some edible flowers such as nasturtiums, violets or chive blossoms.

Preparation:

1. Bring a large pot of salted water to a boil. Submerge the lobsters headfirst, cover and simmer for 10-12 minutes depending on the size of the lobsters. Remove the lobsters from the water and set aside to cool. Discard the water.
2. Once cool enough to handle, break off the claws, knuckles, legs and tail. Remove the meat and cut into bite size pieces.
3. Combine the shallot, tarragon, parsley, salt and pepper, oil, lemon juice, and vinegar in a wide mouth jar, cover and shake until well blended.

To serve: Arrange the lettuce on the plates, divide the lobster meat and place in the middle of each plate and drizzle with the vinaigrette. Arrange the tomatoes, tarragon sprigs and flowers around the exterior for a colorful border and presentation.

Riddle: Larry the lobster was afraid his partner

Tarra had left him. Larry could not find Tarra

anywhere. So, he called up one of their friends

and asked if they knew where Tarra was.

What did the friend reply?

Answer: Tarra Gone

MAIN DISHES

AND PASTAS

Lobster can be used in a variety of main dishes, pastas and risottos. Here are some time-tested recipes and some innovative ways to incorporate lobster into your meals.

Riddle: What did Larry the lobster say to his friend Clarissa the cow before he took her picture?

Answer: Say Cheese.

LOBSTER MAC AND CHEESE

Level 1: Simple Lobster Baked Mac and Cheese with lobster.

Step 1: 2 boxes of Annie's organic mac and cheese or similar

Step 2: Follow the instructions for preparation on the box but cook the pasta two minutes less than instructed so that it is still "al dente" and not mushy.

Step 3: Warm a skillet with 1 tablespoon butter and 1/2 cup cubed Velveeta cheese. Once melted add bite size cooked lobster meat (tails and claws of two 1 ¼ pound lobsters) to the skillet. Gently mix and then add to the prepared mac and cheese.

Step 4: Preheat the oven to 375 degrees.

Step 5: Spray an 8x11 or similar size oven proof dish with nonstick cooking spray (preferably olive oil) and gently spoon the lobster and mac and cheese mixture into the pan.

Step 6: Sprinkle with Panko breadcrumbs and bake uncovered for 20 minutes or until bubbly and the top is golden brown.
Serve with a salad, steamed broccoli or other vegetable.

Level 2: Adult version
Same as above only add ¼ cup white wine or sherry to the lobster, butter and Velveeta cheese mixture.

Level 3: Master Chef version – Take your time with this one.

Ingredients

- 6 small fresh lobster tails (1 1/2 pounds total)
- 8 tbsps (4 oz.) unsalted butter, divided, plus more for greasing baking dish
- 1 small (5 oz.) yellow onion, sliced (3/4 cup)
- 3 garlic cloves, sliced
- 1 (6-inch) thyme sprig, plus thyme leaves for garnish
- 1 cup dry white wine
- 2 cups whole milk
- 1 cup heavy whipping cream
- 2 (6-inch) tarragon sprigs, plus tarragon leaves for garnish
- 1 pound uncooked short curly pasta (such as cavatappi or campanelle)
- ½ tsp paprika
- ⅓ cup (about 1 1/2 oz.) all-purpose flour
- 12 oz. fontina cheese (preferably Fontina Val d›Aosta), grated (about 3 cups)
- 6 oz. Gruyère cheese, grated (about 1 1/2 cups)
- 8 oz. mascarpone cheese
- 1 ½ tsps soy sauce
- ½ tsp black pepper
- ½ tsp ground mustard
- ⅛ tsp ground nutmeg
- ¾ cup panko (Japanese-style breadcrumbs)
- 1 ounce Parmesan cheese, grated (about 1/4 cup)
- 1 tsp grated lemon zest (from 1 lemon)

Preparation

1. Grease a 3-quart, 13- x 9-inch baking dish with butter; set aside. Bring a large pot of salted water to a boil over medium-high. Add lobster tails; cook, undisturbed, until shells turn red but meat is still slightly translucent, about 2 minutes (lobster should be undercooked). Using tongs, transfer lobster to a large bowl; let cool 5 minutes. Transfer 2 cups of the cooking water to a heatproof measuring cup and set aside; reserve remaining water in pot on stovetop. Using kitchen shears, and working over the bowl to catch any juices, cut down the center of each lobster

tail shell, transfer meat to a cutting board, and add shells to bowl. Remove and discard digestive tract from the lobster tails. Chop lobster meat into 1-inch pieces and place in a medium bowl; cover and refrigerate.

2. Melt 2 tablespoons of the butter in a large saucepan over medium-high. Add reserved lobster shells with any juices from bowl; cook, stirring often, until aromatic, about 2 minutes. Add onion, garlic, and thyme sprig; cook, stirring often, until onion is soft and translucent, about 3 minutes. Add wine; cook, stirring often, until almost dry, about 6 minutes. Stir in reserved 2 cups cooking water in measuring glass, and bring to a simmer over medium. Simmer, stirring occasionally, until reduced by half, about 15 minutes. Stir in milk, cream, and tarragon sprigs; cook over medium-low, stirring occasionally, 10 minutes. Remove from heat. Pour through a fine mesh strainer into a large heatproof bowl; discard solids. There should be about 4 cups lobster stock; set aside. Wipe saucepan clean; set aside. Preheat oven to 400°F.

3. While lobster stock reduces, return remaining lobster cooking water in large pot to a boil over high. Add pasta and cook for 1 minute less than package instructions for slightly less than al dente. Drain and set aside.

4. Melt 4 tablespoons of the butter in cleaned saucepan over medium until foamy. Whisk in flour; cook, whisking constantly, until bubbly and light golden brown, about 2 minutes. Gradually whisk in reserved 4 cups strained milk mixture. Cook, whisking often, until thickened, 6 to 8 minutes. Remove from heat; gradually whisk in fontina and Gruyère, whisking until melted. Add mascarpone and whisk until smooth. Stir in soy sauce, pepper, mustard, and nutmeg. Gently stir in cooked pasta and lobster meat. Spoon mixture into prepared baking dish; set aside.

5. Microwave remaining 2 tablespoons butter in a medium-size microwavable bowl on HIGH until melted, about 30 seconds. Stir in panko, Parmesan, lemon zest, and paprika. Sprinkle evenly over mac and cheese mixture in baking dish. Bake in preheated oven until bubbly and light golden on top, about 20 minutes. Remove from oven; let stand 10 minutes. Garnish with thyme leaves and tarragon leaves. Serve

CLASSIC LOBSTER THERMIDOR (YIELDS 4)

This easy Lobster Thermidor is a restaurant quality lobster recipe you can make at home in less than an hour. It is simple, a little decadent and perfect with a creamy cognac sauce.

Ingredients:

- 2 1 1/2 to 1 3/4-pound cooked Maine lobsters
- 2 tbsps unsalted butter
- 2 tbsps minced shallots
- 1/2 tsp minced garlic
- 2 tbsps all-purpose flour
- 2 tbsps cognac or brandy
- 3/4 cup milk
- 1/4 cup heavy cream
- 1/4 tsp salt, *plus 1/8 tsp*

- 1/8 tsp ground white pepper
- 1/2 cup finely grated Parmesan, *plus 2 tbsps*
- 1 tbsp dry mustard powder
- 1 tbsp finely chopped fresh tarragon leaves
- 2 tsps finely chopped parsley, *plus additional for garnish*
- 1/4 cup shredded gruyere cheese

Preparation:

1. Preheat the oven to 375° F. Line a baking sheet with aluminum foil and set aside.
2. Cut the lobsters in half lengthwise with a sharp knife and remove the tail meat.
3. Twist off the claws from the body and gently crack with the back of a heavy knife to remove the meat. Gently pull the front legs from the shell and discard.
4. Chop the tail meat and claw meat into bite sized pieces and set aside.
5. Place the halved lobster shells on the baking sheet and set aside.
6. Melt the butter in a deep skillet over medium heat. Add the shallots and garlic, stirring, until fragrant, about 30 seconds. Add the flour and whisk to combine.
7. Cook the flour mixture, stirring constantly to make a light roux, approximately 2 minutes.
8. Add the cognac and cook for 10 seconds, stirring constantly.

9. Slowly add the milk, stirring constantly to combine. Bring to a boil, reduce the heat, and simmer until thick enough to coat the back of a spoon, approximately 2 to 3 minutes.
10. Slowly add the cream, stirring constantly, until thoroughly combined. Continue cooking while stirring over medium heat for 1 minute. (The mixture will be very thick.) Season with salt and pepper.
11. Remove from the heat and stir in the parmesan cheese, mustard, tarragon, and parsley. Fold in the lobster meat.
12. Divide the mixture among the lobster shells and place stuffed side up on a clean baking sheet.
13. Sprinkle the top of each lobster with the gruyere and broil until the top is golden brown, 5 minutes.
14. Place 1 lobster half on each plate, garnish with additional parsley, and serve immediately.

LOBSTER NEWBURG

History of Lobster Newberg – Lobster a la Wenberg

Lobster Newberg is an American classic dish that is sure to impress everyone you serve it to. It is a rich, creamy, saucy, and unbelievably delicious, elegant entree for any special occasion. There is more than one claim to the history of Lobster Newberg. The claims are a little confusing, as the dates do not seem to come out right. But here is what I have collected from "What's Cooking America". https://whatscookingamerica. net/history/lobsternewberghistory.htm

Did you know that it was among the most popular dishes served in the American Pavilion at the Paris Exposition of 1900.

Also, as I put in the history of lobster section is was included on the New York Central Train Systems dining service menu for $2.25.

Photo from Taste of Home magazine, March/April 2003

1867 – Some historians believe that Lobster Newberg originated at the Hotel Fauchere in Milford, PA, as Lobster Newberg was the signature dish of this elegant hotel during the 1800s. Louis Fauchere, known locally as the "crazy Frenchman," purchased a small saloon, (known as the "Van Gorden & La Bar" and also previously known as "The French Hotel" which is believed to have been owned by relatives of his wife, Rosalie Perrochet Fauche, who had come to Milford as part of the French settlement in the early 19th century. He left his position as chef at New York City's famous Delmonico's restaurant to open this hotel and dining room, also called Delmonico's.

He originally built the hotel summer retreat for New York City society. Louis Fauchere prided himself on the hotel's original cuisine and an elegant atmosphere, and the restaurant soon became famous. He always claimed he invented Lobster Newberg, but this has not ever been proven. He worked at Delmonico's Restaurant under the famous chef, Alessandro Filippini, who worked there from 1849 to 1888. Louis Fauchere left Delmonico's Restaurant and permanently moved to Milford in 1867. Fauchere opened the Hotel Fauchere eight years before Delmonico's Restaurant claimed it was created in 1876. You be the judge!

Caesar Chiappini, master chef of the Hotel Fauchere for 42 years (1926-1968), is given credit for perfecting and popularizing the dish with his own secret recipe.

1876 – The most popular theory on the history of the dish was created at the Delmonico's Restaurant in New York City. The first Delmonico's restaurant was opened in 1827 by brothers Giovanni and Pietro Delmonico. The brothers hired French cooks of ability from the steady stream of immigrants who settled in New York.

Lobster Newberg was originally introduced and named after Ben Wenberg, a wealthy sea captain engaged in the fruit trade between Cuba and New York. When on shore, he customarily ate at Delmonico's Restaurant. One day in 1876, home from a cruise, he entered the cafe and announced that he had brought back a new way to cook lobster (where he originally got the idea for this new dish has never been discovered). Calling for a blazer (chafing dish), he demonstrated his discovery by cooking the dish at the table and invited Charles Delmonico to taste it. Delmonico said, "Delicious" and forthwith entered the dish on the restaurant menu, naming it in honor of its creator <u>Lobster a</u>

la Wenberg. The dish quickly became popular and much in demand, especially by the after-theater clientele.

Many months after Ben Wenberg and Charles Delmonico fought or argued over an as-yet-undiscovered and probably trivial matter. The upshot was that Charles banished Wenberg from Delmonico's and ordered Lobster a la Wenberg struck from the menu. That did not stop patrons from asking for the dish. By typographical slight-of-hand, Delmonico changed the spelling from "Wenberg" to "Newberg," and Lobster Newberg was born. This dish has also been called Lobster Delmonico.

Delmonico's famous chef, Chef Charles Ranhofer (1936-1899), altered the original recipe to add his own touch. In 1876, Charles Ranhofer retired and returned to France. In 1879, three years after he left Delmonico's to retire in France, Charles Ranhofer returned to America and Delmonico's as chef de cuisine at the 26th Street (Madison Square) restaurant. He was the chef at Delmonico's from 1862 to 1896. In his book, The Epicurean, published in 1894, Ranhofer gives the following recipe for Lobster a la Newberg:

"Cook six lobsters each weighing about two pounds in boiling salted water for twenty-five minutes. Twelve pounds of live lobster when cooked yields from two to two and a half pounds of meat with three to four ounces of coral. When cold detach the bodies from the tails and cut the latter into slices, put them into a sautoir, each piece lying flat, and add hot clarified butter; season with salt and fry lightly on both sides without coloring; moisten to their height with good raw cream; reduce quickly to half; and then add two or three spoonful's of Madeira wine; boil the liquid once more only, then remove and thicken with a thickening of egg yolks and raw cream. Cook without boiling, incorporating a little cayenne and butter; then arrange the pieces in a vegetable dish and pour the sauce over."

In the **1880's**, it was the favorite lobster specialty at the resort hotels on Coney Island. The hotels are reported to have bought as much as 3,500 pounds of lobster daily during the peak season to satisfy customer demand.

LOBSTER NEWBERG RECIPE:

Ingredients

- 5 tbsps unsalted butter
- 2 cups cooked lobster meat, cut into 1/2-inch pieces*
- 1 tsp salt
- 1 cup heavy cream, divided
- 3 egg yolks
- 1/4 tsp Tabasco or 1/8 tsps cayenne pepper or to taste
- 1/3 cup cognac, sherry, brandy, or Madeira (your choice)
- Toast Points

Preparation

1. In a large frying pan or chafing dish over medium-low heat, heat butter until the foam begins to subside. Immediately add the cooked lobster meat and saute, turning all the pieces, for approximately 2 minutes.
2. Add 3/4 cup of the cream and add the salt; stir and simmer for an additional 2 minutes (do not allow the mixture to boil).
3. Meanwhile in another bowl, beat the remaining 1/4 cup of cream together with the egg yolks.
4. Stir in the Tabasco (I prefer Frank's hot sauce) and cognac to the lobster mixture. Stir or whisk in a few tablespoons of the simmering cream mixture into the egg/cream mixture. Reduce heat to low and stir the mixture until thickened (but not boiling).
5. Remove from heat and serve immediately on Toast Points.
6. Makes 2 to 4 servings.

LOBSTER ETOUFFEE

This flavorful staple of Cajun and Creole cooking is an iconic dish that encapsulates the warmth and vivaciousness of Louisiana and its people. I found this history and background in "Recette Magazine".

History of Etouffee

The exact origins of etouffee are difficult to pinpoint. Culinary historians believe the dish was first served to diners in Breaux Bridge, Louisiana in the 1950s, but it may have been around much earlier than that. The prevailing local lore traces the earliest recipe back to the Hebert Hotel in the 1920s. The recipe was adapted and served by Aline Champagne at the Rendezvous Restaurant just outside of Breaux Bridge. The dish was a hit with locals and tourists, eventually rising to the iconic status it has today. **Etoufee can be made with any shellfish. For this recipe we are using lobster.**

https://blog.suvie.com/everything-to-know-about-etouffee#:~:text=The%20 exact%20origins%20of%20etouffee,Hebert%20Hotel%20in%20the%201920s.

Taste of Etouffee

Etouffee is rich and spicy with the sweet and briny flavor of shellfish. The shellfish is coated in a velvety thick gravy flavored with traditional Cajun or Creole seasonings. The dish is typically served over rice, which soaks up the lush etouffee sauce.

Creole vs. Cajun Etouffee

Etouffee can be found in both Creole and Cajun cuisine, with slight but important differences in the seasoning and preparation of each version. Creole etouffee uses a traditional French-style roux made from butter and flour while the roux for Cajun etouffee is made with oil, lard, or other animal fats. Cajun etouffee is also spicier, featuring more peppers and ground spices than the Creole version, which is more herbaceous. Additionally, Creole etouffee is sometimes made with tomatoes, an ingredient generally absent in Cajun cuisine.

How Etouffee is Made

The word etouffee in French literally translates to "smothered" and is a reference to the cooking technique used to make the dish. Smothering is essentially a form of stove-top braising, wherein the meat and vegetables are browned in a pan then deglazed and simmered until tender.

Etouffee is made primarily with shellfish and the "holy trinity" of vegetables – onion, celery, and bell pepper. The shellfish and vegetables are simmered in a blond roux with herbs and spices until the meat is cooked through and the sauce is thick. Serve your etouffee with Creole Red Beans and Rice.

LOBSTER ETOUFFEE RECIPE

This recipe is a combination of both cajun and creole etouffee recipes. It uses Cajun seasoning, butter and oil as opposed to lard and includes tomatoes. This recipe is adapted from Paula Deen and Emeril Lagassee.

Ingredients

- ¼ cup oil
- ¼ cup butter plus 4 tbsps butter reserved
- ½ cup flour plus extra flour as needed to form a paste
- 1 ½ cup chopped yellow onion
- 1 cup chopped celery
- ½ cup chopped green bell pepper
- 3 garlic cloves minced
- 2 bay leaves
- ½ tsp black pepper
- ½ tsp white pepper
- ½ tsp cayenne pepper or to taste
- 1 tsp Cajun seasoning or to taste
- 3-5 dashes hot sauce or to taste
- 1 8- ounce jar clam juice
- 1 14.5- ounce can diced tomatoes
- 3 cups chicken stock
- 1 tsp salt
- 1 pound or 4 cups langostinos can substitute crawfish or shrimp
- ½ cup minced green onions plus extra for garnish
- ½ cup minced fresh parsley leaves

Preparation

1. To make the roux, melt butter with oil in a large heavy saucepan over low heat. Whisk flour into the oil to form a paste and cooking over low heat and whisk continuously, until the mixture turns a caramel color and gives off a nutty aroma, about 15 to 20 minutes.
2. Add the onion, green pepper, celery, and garlic and cook over low heat until the vegetables are limp, about 5 minutes.
3. Add the black pepper, white pepper, cayenne pepper, Cajun seasoning, green onions, parsley, and hot sauce to taste.

4. Add clam juice, chicken broth, tomatoes with their juice and salt to taste. Bring to a boil, reduce the heat to low and simmer for 10 to 15 minutes until mixture thickens.
5. Add lobster meat and cook for 3-5 minutes careful not to overcook. Remove from heat and add the 4 tablespoons reserved butter and stir to melt. Garnish with the green onions, parsley and serve over steamed rice.

Riddle: Why doesn't Larry the Lobster play basketball?

Answer: He doesn't like being stuffed.

LOCKE-OBER'S LOBSTER SAVANNAH RECIPE

This is a classic baked lobster dish from the famous and now closed Boston landmark restaurant Locke-Obers. I can assure you it has stood the test of time (decades, in fact!) and deserves a place at your table if you have any love whatsoever for this rich, delicious crustacean!

Ingredients:

- 4 2-pound lobsters, cooked and cooled
- 2 tbsps butter
- 12 large white mushrooms, chopped into 1/2-inch pieces
- 3 shallots peeled and finely chopped
- 1/2 red bell pepper, chopped into 1/2-inch pieces.
- 1/4 cup brandy
- 1/2 cup cream sherry
- 2 cups heavy cream
- Pinch of paprika
- Salt and freshly ground black pepper
- Juice of half a lemon, or to taste
- 1/4 cup finely grated Parmigiano-Reggiano cheese

Preparation:

1. Remove lobster claws and knuckles, crack them open and reserve meat. Using heavy kitchen shears, cut a long 1 ½ inch- wide rectangle out of the top of each lobster body, extending from about 2 inches behind eyes to about 1 inch from tail. Keeping body in one piece, carefully pry meat from tail, and set aside. Remove any meat from body cavity, as well as the green tomalley (liver), and set aside. Rinse lobster bodies and reserve.

2. Preheat oven to 400 degrees. Cut lobster meat into 1-inch chunks, and set aside in a bowl with tomalley. Place a large sauté pan over high heat, and melt butter. Add mushrooms, and stir until mushrooms begin to release their juices, 1 to 2 minutes. Add shallots and red pepper, and stir until liquid has vaporated and vegetables begin to brown.

3. Remove pan from heat, and add brandy and sherry. Carefully touch a lighted match to mixture to flame it. When flames subside, place pan over medium-high heat. Add heavy cream, paprika and salt and pepper to taste. Add lobster meat and tomalley to pan, and stir. Add lemon juice, and adjust seasonings to taste. Allow sauce to simmer until lobster is heated and sauce is slightly thickened, about 5 minutes.

4. Place reserved lobster bodies in a large baking pan. Place equal portions of lobster mixture in cavities of

5. bodies, and sprinkle with Parmigiano-Reggiano. Bake until cheese is lightly browned, 2 to 3 minutes. Serve immediately.

THE HIRSHON MINORCAN LOBSTER STEW – CALDERETA DE LANGOSTA

Caldereta De Minorca is from one of the Balearic Islands located in the Mediterranean Sea belonging to Spain. Its name derives from its size, contrasting it with nearby Majorca. I was served this stew on a trip to Spain and have since made it with local Maine lobsters or large whole shrimp. It is delightful.

Ingredients

- Two 1 ½–pound female Minorcan lobsters (Spiny or Maine lobsters or large whole shrimp with heads and shells attached)
- ½ cup extra-virgin olive oil
- 1 large Spanish onion, cut into ¼-inch dice
- 2 plum tomatoes, coarsely chopped
- 2 large green cubanelle peppers (preferred) or use green bell peppers, cut into slices
- 4 garlic cloves, thinly sliced
- Sea salt and freshly ground black pepper
- 1 Bay leaf
- 1 liter shellfish stock (preferred) or use the water reserved from the lobsters

Topping

- Reserved roe from the lobsters, if they have any
- 3 garlic cloves, cut into thin slices
- 1 large bunch of parsley, leaves removed and chopped finely
- 10 almonds, toasted
- 4 saffron threads
- ½ lemon, juiced
- ¼ cup bran

Preparation

1. Boil the lobsters in salted water for 10 minutes. Remove the lobsters and reserve the water if not using shellfish stock.
2. Separate the heads and cut the tails into slices. Cut the heads in half, lengthwise and clean the lobsters, getting rid of the intestines. If they have roe, carefully remove and reserve for topping.
3. In a mortar and pestle, crush the cooked lobster roe, garlic, parsley, almonds and saffron.
4. When mixed, add the lemon juice and brandy. This is reserved until the end.
5. Heat the oil in a casserole dish (preferably earthenware). Sauté the onions, peppers, garlic and a little parsley. Simmer for 10 minutes.
6. Add the tomatoes and cook for 15 minutes, until the sauce thickens.
7. Pass the sauce through a sieve and place back in the dish.
8. Add the chopped lobster, bay leaf and the shellfish stock, or the water reserved from the lobsters.
9. Cook for 10 minutes over a low heat.
10. Add the topping mixture and simmer for another 5 minutes. Serve immediately with thin, toasted slices of a good country bread or a baguette to dunk in the sauce.

FLAMING LOBSTER WITH COGNAC CREAM

This is a wonderful treat for Valentines Day or any dinner to impress a partner, family or friends.

Ingredients:

- 1 large lobster, 2-3 pounds
- 4 tbsps butter
- 1 shallot minced
- 2 tbsps minced parsley
- Salt and pepper to taste
- ½ cup cognac, warmed
- 4 tbsps heavy cream

Preparation:

1. Split lobster in half lengthwise, remove sac and intestinal track. Place on an ovenproof baking dish just large enough to hold the lobster. Mix butter with shallot, parley, salt and pepper and spread over lobster. Bake in a preheated oven at 450 degrees for 15 minutes.
2. Remove from oven and place in an open space on the stove or heat proof counter. Pour warmed cognac over the lobster and carefully light. Pour the cream over the lobster and return to the oven to blend the juices for a few minutes. Serve one half lobster for each person and drizzle the cognac sauce over the body.

Serve this dish with a simple or elegant side of your choice such as roasted corn, asparagus, green beans or a combination of roasted vegetables.

ASIAN LOBSTER ROLLS WITH ROSEMARY GINGER VINAIGRETTE

This is a wonderful fusion of East meets West that is relatively easy to make, healthy and a treat for your taste buds.

Ingredients for the rolls

- 3 large zucchinis (they need to be large enough that you can slice them length wise and then roll them)
- 2 cooked 8-oz lobster tails, shelled, halved lengthwise and thinly sliced crosswise (you can use shrimp, sashimi or crab too).
- ¾ cup sprouts (alfalfa, daikon, watercress)
- 24 1-inch pieces of thinly sliced pickled ginger

Ingredients for the viniaigrette

- 3 tbsps soy sauce
- 2 tbsps wine vinegar
- 1 tbsp sherry
- 2 tbsps honey
- 1 ½ tbsp minced fresh ginger.
- 1 ½ tbsps minced fresh rosemary
- ½ tsp crushed red pepper
- ½ cup vegetable oil

Preparation:

1. Place 1 zucchini on a cutting board. Using a sharp vegetable peeler, cut the zucchini into thin ribbon about 5 inches long and 1 ½ inches wide. Repeat with the remaining zucchini, making a total of 12 ribbons.
2. Divide lobster meat equally, placing a piece on the end of each zucchini ribbon. Top with sprouts and pickled ginger. Starting at the filled end, roll each piece of zucchini into a cylinder. Place seam side down on a paper towel-lined baking sheet. Cover and chill for at least 2 hours.
3. Prepare vinaigrette by whisking everything except the oil in a medium bowl to blend. Gradually add oil. To serve, pour vinaigrette in a small bowl, place in cent of platter and surround with lobster rolls.

This dish can be served as an appetizer or as a main dish with steamed or fried rice.

NEW ENGLAND LOBSTER STEW

Ingredients:

- 1 pound fresh lobster meat
- 6 tbsps butter
- 6 cups half and half
- Salt and pepper to taste
- Cayenne pepper to taste (optional)
- Freshly chopped parsley.

- 1-2 tbsps sherry to taste (optional)
- 4 slices of ciabatta buttered and toasted (alternatively toast, rub with fresh garlic before buttering)
- 4 lemon wedges

Preparation:

1. Melt butter in a large saucepan. Add lobster and gently sauté on low heat for 2 to 3 minutes until butter nice and pink.
2. Add cream and sherry (optional). Simmer for 5 minutes. Add seasoning and taste. Adjust as needed.
3. Remove half of the lobster meat to a small bowl for reserve. Keep warm.
4. Ladle stew in 4 serving dishes equally dividing the lobstering each bowl. Float a piece of toasted ciabatta on top of each bowl and top with reserved lobster and parsley. Serve with a wedge of lemon .

SOUTH OF THE BORDER LOBSTER

Ingredients:

- 4 1 ½ pound lobsters
- 8 tbsps (1 stick) salted butter
- 2 cloves fresh garlic minced
- Juice of 2 limes
- ¼ cup fresh cilantro, chopped
- ½ tsp cumin
- Dash of favorite hot sauce to taste

Preparation:

1. In a large pot, bring 2 inches of water to a boil with a pinch of salt. Add the lobsters, and cover and steam for 10 minutes.
2. Once the lobsters are cooked remove, carefully crack the claws with a cleaver, gently slice the underside shell of tail and plate. This will make it easier to remove the meat from the shell.
3. While the lobsters are cooking, melt butter in a small saucepan. Sauté the garlic for one minute being careful not to brown.
4. Add the lime juice, cilantro and cumin, seasoning with hot sauce to taster. Divide the dipping sauce into 4 small bowls and serve one with each lobster. Garnish with cilantro and extra wedges of lime.

CRUSTLESS CAPE COD LOBSTER PIE

Ingredients:

Filling

- 6 tbsps butter
- 6 tbsps flour
- 1 cup milk, warmed
- 2 cups half-and-half
- 1 lb. fresh lobster meat
- 1 tsp paprika
- ⅓ cup sherry
- Pinch cayenne pepper or more to taste
- 2 tbsps fresh chopped parsley
- ½ tsp salt

Lobster Pie Topping

- ¾ cup panko or breadcrumbs
- 4 tbsps butter, melted
- ½ cup finely crushed kettle cooked plain potato chips
- 2 tbsps freshly grated parmesan cheese
- ¾ tsp paprika

Preparation:

1. Preheat the oven to 375 degrees.
2. In a 2-quart saucepan, melt 4 tablespoons butter over low heat. Do not boil. Add flour and cook, stirring, for 2-3 minutes. Whisk warm milk and half and half into the flour mixture and simmer for 10 minutes stirring constantly until thickened.
3. In a separate sauté pan, melt remaining 2 tablespoons of butter. Add lobster meat, sprinkle with paprika and cook over low heat for 5 minutes, until butter is nice and pink. Add sherry, a pinch or 2 of cayenne pepper, chopped parsley and salt.
4. Gently fold the lobster and butter mixture into the cream sauce and stir to mix thoroughly. Divide the lobster and sauce equally into four individual casserole or large ramekin dishes. Sprinkle with the topping and a little more paprika and a squirt of lemon and bake uncovered for 12-15 minutes until golden brown and bubbly.
5. Serve with a side of choice and warm crusty bread.

NEW ENGLAND BAKED STUFFED LOBSTER

This is a New England favorite. Families and lobster shacks have different versions. I particularly like my recipe below.

Ingredients:

- 2 1 ½ pound lobsters
- 1 ½ cups Ritz cracker crumbs
- 2 tbsps freshly grated Romano cheese
- ½ tsp oregano
- ½ tsp basil
- 1 tbsp fresh chopped parsley
- Salt, pepper and a dash of hot sauce to taste
- ½ stick of butter sliced into 8 pieces
- Juice of 1 large lemon
- Paprika

Preparation:

1. Split the lobsters lengthwise on the underside. Remove sac and intestinal vein. Leave the tamale or roe in cavity if desired. Crack the claws and slit the inner shell of the tail in 3 diagonal cuts to prevent curling.
2. Toss the remaining ingredient together and fill each lobster body. Place two slices of butter on each lobster half, drizzle with lemon juice and sprinkle with paprika. These may be made ahead, wrapped tightly and refrigerated for up to two hours. If making in advance do not drizzle the lemon juice on the lobsters until you are ready to cook.
3. Bake in an oven preheated to 400 degrees for 20 minutes and serve with bowls of hot lemon butter and hot sauce to taste.

BOURBON LOBSTER

Ingredients:

- 1 ½ pounds fresh uncooked and diced lobster meat (tail, claws, knuckles)
- 1 red bell pepper julienned (cut into thin strips)
- 4 tbsps butter
- ¼ cup bourbon
- 1 cup white wine
- 1 cup cream
- 1 tbsp Cajun seasoning
- 2 tbsps Cajun seasoning
- 2 tbsps chopped parsley
- Chopped scallions and paprika to garnish.

Preparation:

1. Melt butter in a sauté pan. Add peppers and sauté over medium heat for two minutes. Add diced raw lobster meat and bourbon. Raise the heat and carefully ignite the bourbon to flambe the lobster meat for 10-15 seconds or until the bourbon cooks off. Reduce the heat to low medium and remove the lobster from the pan and set aside and cover.

2. Add white wine, cream Cajun season and parsley to the pan and simmer, stirring until the sauce thickens. Do not leave your sauce. Once thickened add the lobster meat back to the pan to heat through to meld flavors. Serve over white rice and top with a few chopped scallions and a dusting of cayenne or paprika depending on taste.

MADHUR JAFFREY'S LOBSTER KERALA STYLE

This recipe is from the award-winning chef and author Madhur Jaffrey's book "An Invitation to Indian Cooking". This book should be a staple in any home chef's library interested in the recipes from the sub-continent.

Ingredients:

- 3 tbsps vegetable oil
- 2 medium-sized onions, peeled and finely chopped
- A piece of fresh ginger, about ¾ inch cube, peeled
- 4 cloves garlic, peeled and chopped
- ½ cup grated and roasted fresh coconut
- ½ tsp ground turmeric
- 1 tbsp ground coriander, roasted
- ¼ tsp cayenne pepper
- 3 tbsps tamarind paste
- ½ cup tomato sauce
- 2 pounds uncooked lobster meat cut in 1-inch pieces

Preparation:

1. Heat oil in a heavy bottomed 10-inch skillet over medium-high heat. Put in the chopped onions and fry, stirring, for 7-8 minutes or until the onions are slightly browned, but soft. Turn of the heat
2. In a blender combine the ginger, garlic, and grated roasted coconut. Blend at high speed until tiny grains are formed. Add contents of blender to the skillet. Also add the turmeric coriander, cayenne, tamarind paste, tomato sauce, salt, and ½ cup water. Bring to a boil. Cover, lower heat, and simmer gently for 5 minutes.
3. Seven to 8 minutes before serving, bring the sauce to a boil. Add the lobster, fold in, and cook at high temperature, stirring continuously until the meat turns opaque (about 5 minutes(. The sauce should be very thick and cling to the meat.
4. Place in a warm bowl and serve with a rice dish or naans and some kind of dal. Mansoor Dal with vegetables is a good recommendation.

TAJ MAHAL LOBSTER

I had a version of this dish on a trip to India years ago. It was made with spiny lobsters. I have adapted the recipe for Atlantic lobsters. Either way the exotic flavors are exquisite and do not overpower the sweetness of the lobster. If you want a taste of India, I highly recommend experimenting with this one. This recipe serves two.

Ingredients:

- 2 1 ½ pound lobsters
- Pulp from 1/2 fresh coconut, or 1/3 cup unsweetened coconut milk
- 1 fresh hot green chili, seeded
- 2 garlic cloves, minced
- ½ piece fresh ginger root, peeled
- 6 stems fresh coriander with leaves, plus sprigs for garnish
- 2 tbsps Balsamic vinegar
- ¼ tsp slat
- 1 tbsp olive oil
- 2 lemon twists or slices

Preparation:

1. Steam the lobsters in 1 inch of boiling slated water. Cover and cook for 10 minutes. When cool enough to handle, split them open and remove the tail, knuckle and claw meat trying to keep the pieces in tack. Snip the legs off the body.
2. To make the sauce, combine the coconut, garlic chili, ginger root, coriander, vinegar and slat in a food processor and blend to a paste. To serve, arrange lobster meat in the center of two serving plates. Spoon the sauce on top and drizzle with olive oil. Arrange the legs around the of each plate and garnish with cilantro sprigs and lemon.

JP'S SIGNATURE LOBSTER LINGUINE

This is one of my own recipes that I have modified and experimented with over the years. I make it every summer in Rockport, and it is always well received by family and friends. I will include the variations so think of this recipe as a treasure map. You can travel the options to lead you to your own culinary pot of lobster gold.

Ingredients

- 2 lobsters 1 ¼ to 1 ½ lbs.
- ¼ cup butter (1 stick)
- 2 cloves garlic
- 1 carrot, 1 stalk of celery and 1 onion quartered.
- Fresh chopped cayenne peppers to taste or if unavailable substitute with flakes or powdered cayenne peppers to taste. Don't overdo it or it will detract from the balance of the other flavors.
- 4-6 fresh Roma tomatoes seeded and diced or a can of crushed Roma tomatoes.
- 2 tbsps olive oil
- ¼ cup white wine or vegetable broth or to taste
- 2 tbsps of tomato paste
- 1 cup mornay sauce, bechamel sauce, heavy cream or crème fraiche (see instructions to guide your choices)
- 2 cups reserved lobster stock or vegetable stock
- 1 packet of good quality Italian linguine or homemade if you have the time.
- 1 shallot

Preparation:

1. Boil lobsters in a rolling boiling salted pot of water for no more than 10 minutes. Remember the most humane (which to me sounds like an oxymoron since we are cooking lobster not humans) is to put them in the freezer for 10-20 minutes to numb their senses. Once cooked remove the tail, claws and knuckles and set aside to cool. The alternative is to buy the whole fresh lobster and have it steamed or boiled at your fish market or grocery store providing that service.
2. Once cooled to touch remove the tail claws and knuckle meat from the lobsters and reserve.

3. Place the shells and the body of the lobster back into the water. Add the roughly cut carrot, celery and onion to the pot and bring to a boil. Boil for 10 to 15 minutes to extract the flavors and then strain reserving the stock. Place the lobster stock back in the pot and keep warm. This is the water you will use to cook the linguine.

4. To prepare your sauce, pour 1-2 tablespoons of olive oil in a heavy deep sided skillet and place on medium – high heat until shimmering but not smoking. Add your finely chopped shallots, chopped clove of garlic and cayenne pepper and simmer until shallots and garlic are soft but not brown. Add the tomatoes and white wine. Once bubbling, turn down the heat to let the sauce simmer for 5 minutes. Add the tomato past and stir. Keep on low heat. Next gently stir in your choice of mornay sauce, bechamel sauce, heavy cream or crème fraiche. They are all excellent options but each one offers a different flavor component. I always add a little sherry which is a classic addition to any recipe with cream and lobster. I suggest you taste as you go to decide on salt, wine, sherry or spices. You are the culinary scientist, and this is your experiment. If, however, you do not have the time to complete step 4 you can substitute a really good quality marinara sauce and add some cream or crème fraiche, wine and any addition spices (cayenne) you might like to personalize your sauce.

5. Now bring your pasta stock to a boil, taste for salt. It should have a sea water saltiness. Add more if necessary. Next cut your lobster tail and knuckles and claws into bite size pieces while reserving the thumb of the claw to garnish.

6. In a separate skillet melt the butter, squeeze the juice of one lemon into the butter. Once melted and warm add your lobster meat to the butter to keep warm and absorb the flavors.

7. Add your pasta to the boiling water and cook until al dente. DO NOT OVERCOOK. When it is close to being done remove a cup of the stock and set aside.

8. Next fold the lobster and lemon butter sauce into the red sauce and gently stir. Bring to a simmer but don't boil. Add any seasoning adjustments you might want.

9. Strain the pasta and place the pasta in the skillet with the sauce and gently combine to evenly distribute the sauce. Add a little of the reserved lobster stock if necessary. Once combined serve immediately and garnish with fresh chopped parsley and a slice of lemon. Of course, this is your experiment, but I would highly recommend NOT adding cheese to this dish. The richness of ingredients and flavors do not need the distraction of a strong flavored parmigiano or pecorino cheese.

JP'S SIGNATURE LOBSTER AND MUSHROOM LASAGNA WITH TWO SAUCES

This is one of my favorite recipes that I prepare over the Christmas holidays and on other special occasions. You can also combine shrimp or scallops with the lobster to enhance the flavors.

Ingredients:

Spicy Tomato Sauce

- 2 tbsps olive oil
- 1 small onion, finely chopped
- 1 garlic clove, minced
- 1 28-ounce can crushed tomatoes (San Marzano preferred)
- 1 tsp dried basil or ¼ cup finely chopped fresh basil leaves
- ¼ tsp crushed hot red pepper

White-Wine Sauce

- 5 tbsps unsalted butter
- 2 shallots or scallions, minced
- 1/3 cup all-purpose flour
- 1 cup milk
- ½ cup dry white wine
- ½ cup clam juice
- ¼ tsp salt
- ¼ tsp freshly ground white pepper
- Pinch of grated nutmeg
- ½ cup freshly grated parmigiano cheese

Lobster and Mushroom Filling

- 2tbsps olive oil
- 10 oz. fresh mushrooms, sliced
- 2 pounds uncooked lobster meat cut into one-inch pieces
- ½ tsp salt
- ¼ tsp freshly ground white pepper
- 12 oz. fresh spinach lasagna or 9 oz. dried egg lasagna noodles
- 1 tbsp olive oil
- 1 cup grated Swiss or Gruyere cheese
- Chopes fresh basil for garnish

Preparation:

Spicy Tomato Sauce

Heat the oil in a medium saucepan over medium heat. Add the onion and cook, stirring often, until softened, about 4 minutes. Add the garlic and cook for 1 minute. Stir in the tomatoes, basil and red pepper and bring to a simmer. Reduce the heat to low and simmer until thickened, about 45 minutes. (Note: The tomato sauce can be made up to 3 days ahead, cooled, covered and refrigerated.)

White-Wine Sauce

Melt the butter in a heavy-bottomed medium saucepan over low heat. Add the shallots and cook, stirring, until softened, about 2 minutes. Add the flower and let bubble without browning, stirring constantly, about 2 minutes. Whisk in the milk, wine, clam juice, salt, pepper and nutmeg. Simmer, whisking often, until thickened, about 10 minutes. Remove from the heat and whisk in the Parmigiano cheese. (Note: The white sauce can be prepared up to 1 day ahead. Press a piece of plastic wrap directly onto the surface of the sauce to prevent a skin from forming and prick the plastic a few times with a toothpick to allow steam/heat to escape. Once cool, refrigerate.

Lobster-Mushroom filling

Heat the oil in a large skillet over medium-high heat. Add the mushrooms and cook, stirring occasionally, untio they have given off their ligid and are browned, about 10 minutes. Increase the heat to high. Add the lobster, salt and pepper and cooke, stirring often , just until the lobster had turned pink, 1-2 minutes. Transfer the mixture to a medium bowl and let stand for 10 minutes. Drain off the collected juices from the mixture and return the juices to the skillet. Boil the juices over high heat until they are reduced to about 2 tablespoons. Stir the recued juices and white-wine sauce into the seafood mixture.

To Assemble

1. Preheat the oven to 375 degrees F. Lightly butter a 9x13-inch baking dish. In a large pot of lightly salted boiling water, cook the fresh spinach lasagna just unto supple, 1-3 minutes depending on the dryness of the noodles. If using dried noodles cook just until al dente, 8-10 minutes. If using reading cook lasagna noodle move on the next step.

2. Spread ½ cup of the tomato sauce in the bottom of the prepared pan. Lengthwise, arrange four overlapping strips of lasagna noodles. Trim if necessary. Spread half of the lobster-mushroom filling over the noodles, then top with another layer of noodles. Spread with the remaining filling, and top with the remaining noodles. Spread the remaining tomato sauce over the top layer of noodles, then sprinkle with the Gruyere or Swiss cheese. Bake, uncovered, until bubbling, about 30 minutes. Let the lasagna stand for 10 minutes. Just before serving, sprinkle with fresh cut basil.

JP'S SIGNATURE LOBSTER CAKES

I love crab cakes but when I have access to fresh delicate lobster meat during the summer, I make these lobster cakes. They are easy to make and delicious. You can serve them plain with a slice of lemon, on a bed of arugula or other greens, as an open-faced sandwich on a brioche bun or any way you want to enjoy them. You can top your lobster cakes with your favorite condiment or the Lemon-Shallot Vinaigrette (see recipe) if you are serving them over greens. You can also make small cakes as appetizers with a nice aioli or other dipping sauce of choice. I like a light lemon mayonnaise or a mild seafood aioli on the side, so it doesn't overpower the delicate flavor of the lobster.

Ingredients:

- 8 saltine crackers, finely crushed
- 2 tbsps mayonnaise
- ½ tsp Dijon mustard
- ½ tsp seafood seasoning (such as Old Bay)
- ¼ tsp Worcestershire sauce
- 1 egg, beaten
- 1 pinch cayenne pepper (Optional)
- salt to taste
- 1-pound cooked lobster meat padded dry.
- ¼ cup dry breadcrumbs
- 2 tbsps butter

Preparation:

1. Mix crushed crackers, mayonnaise, Dijon, seafood seasoning, Worcestershire sauce, egg, cayenne, and salt together in a large bowl. Add crabmeat and stir until combined but still chunky. Cover and refrigerate for 1 hour.
2. Sprinkle breadcrumbs onto a plate. Shape chilled crab mixture into four small, thick patties. Coat patties completely with breadcrumbs.
3. Melt butter in a skillet over medium heat. Add crab cakes and cook until golden brown, about 4 minutes per side.

LEMON-SHALLOT VINAIGRETTE

This tart, punchy vinaigrette is fantastic on salads, but also is a back-pocket sauce to drizzle over roast chicken, grilled fish, fresh or roasted vegetables, or anything that could use a bright wake-up call.

Ingredients:

- ½ tsp finely grated lemon zest plus 2 tbsps fresh lemon juice
- 2 tbsps minced shallots
- 1 ¼ tsps Dijon mustard
- 1 ¼ tsps white wine vinegar
- 1 small garlic clove (minced)
- ⅓ cup extra-virgin olive oil
- Salt and freshly ground pepper

Preparation:

In a blender, combine the lemon zest and juice, shallots, mustard, vinegar and garlic and puree until smooth. With the machine on, slowly add the olive oil until emulsified. Pour the vinaigrette into a bowl and season with salt and pepper.

JP'S SIGNATURE PENNE ALLA VODKA WITH LOBSTER

Ingredients:

- 12 oz *penne rigate* pasta (also particularly good with spaghetti if you want long pasta)
- 10 oz Fresh lobster cut into bite size pieces
- One small glass of vodka
- 10 oz heavy cream
- ½ orange (untreated and organic), only the peel
- 1 scallion
- 1 tbsp butter
- 1 tbsp extra-virgin olive oil
- Fresh chopped thyme

Preparation:

1. Bring the salted water for the pasta to a boil.
2. Clean the scallion and chop it with a knife.
3. Brown it softly over low heat with the butter and 1 tablespoon of extra-virgin olive oil.
4. Prepare the lobster in bit size pieces.
5. Melt a little butter in the bottom a heavy bottomed skillet with the scallion. Add the vodka until it has warmed and then add the lobster and carefully ignite to flambe the lobster and cook off the vodka. After a few seconds cover the skillet lid to put any remaining flames out. Flambéing is fun and can be a great spectator event if you have the right kitchen and are very careful. It also adds a delicate smokiness to lobster. Reserve a few pieces of the cooked lobster for a garnish.
6. Add the heavy cream and stir to combine and simmer on low heat for 2-3 minutes then cover and remove from the heat.
7. In the meantime, cook the pasta in the boiling salted water.
8. Drain and rinse the pasta 1 min before they are cooked through (al dente). Reserve a cup of the pasta water. Transfer the pasta directly to the pan with the lobster sauce.
9. Allow the pasta to absorb the sauce, stirring continuously. Add a little of the reserved pasta water if needed.

10. Plate the pasta and grate the orange peel on top. I also like grated lemon peel. Either one works fine depending on your preference.
11. Garnish with the fresh chopped thyme and the reserved lobster meat.
12. Serve the pasta immediately.
13. I do not recommend adding any cheese to this pasta because it can overpower and detract from the delicate flavors of the lobster and sauce.

Riddle: What do cat's and lobsters have in common?

Answer: They both have claws.

JP'S LOBSTER FISHER'S PIE
(AKA LOBSTER SHEPARD'S PIE)

I came across this recipe in a well known "non" New England cookbook from a state that borders Vermont. I modified it and changed the name because 1. There is no such thing as a lobster Shepard. Shepards herd sheep, goats, or other small ruminants. Shepard's pie is made with ground lamb. 2. Shepard's Pie is often confused with Cottage Pie which is made with ground beef instead of lamb. So, to put Lobster and Shepard in the same sentence is just an oxymoron. During my last trip to Rockport MA, I went lobster trapping with Captain Jim and his first mate John on their lobster boat "The First Lady." The next day I experimented with the recipe below. How can you go wrong with these ingredients. Give it a try.

Ingredients:

- Five 1 ½ – pound lobsters
- Six large baking potatoes (Maine potatoes preferred)
- 4 large leeks, white and pale green parts only, julienned and washed.
- 1 ½ cups finely diced carrots
- 8 cups shitake mushrooms, stemmed and sliced (porta bella or mild but flavorful mushrooms are fine)

- Sea salt and fresh ground pepper
- 1 cup dry white wine (or cooking sherry if preferred)
- 1 cup heavy cream
- 1 cup half and half
- 7 ½ tbsps unsalted butter
- 4 large shallots minced.
- 1 cup baby peas (fresh or frozen)
- ¼ cup chopped chives

Preparation:

1. Steam lobsters in salted water or sea water about 9 minutes (slightly underdone). Let cool then remove lobster meat, cut into bite size pieces, and set aside.

2. Peel, quarter and boil potatoes until tender. Rice or mash them, add 6 tablespoons butter and half and half. Mash until smooth. Add salt and pepper to taste. You can add a few drops of Frank's hot sauce if you want to add a little heat. Chopped fresh parsley is another nice addition.

3. Melt remaining butter (or mix a little butter with some EVOO) in a large skillet over medium heat. Add the shallots and sauté for 1 minute. Add the leeks and carrots and cook over medium-low heat for 10 minutes. Add mushrooms, season with salt and pepper to taste and cook until mushrooms are tender – about 8-10 minutes.

4. Add the wine (or sherry), bring to a simmer for 3 minutes. Stir in cream and peas and simmer until peas are tender but firm (2-3 minutes max). Remove from the heat. Add the lobster meat and gently combine.

5. Heat oven to 350 degrees. In an oiled or buttered lasagna pan or oval baking dish, spoon the lobster and vegetable mixture into the pan. Gently spread the potatoes evenly over the top. Sprinkle thinly with a mixture of breadcrumbs and freshly grated parmigiano cheese. Finish with paper thin slices of butter.

6. Bake until heated through and topping is golden brown (about 25 minutes). When ready, remove from the oven and top with fresh chopped herbs of choice. I like Italian parsley or chives. Let cool for 5-10 minutes and serve. Cover and refrigerate any leftovers. The flavors will meld with time so may taste even better reheated the next day.

Trapping Lobsters with Captain Jim (background) and First Mate John on the First Lady in Rockport MA.

POACHED LOBSTER IN BEURRE MONTE

This recipe is a dramatic improvement on simply heating already cooked lobster meat in butter to eat alone or in recipes. There are two components to this recipe that are critical to producing delicate, tender, and delicious lobster meat that is not overcooked and rubbery.

Ingredients:

For the Lobster

- As many "live and kicking" lobsters as you choose to cook
- Pot of salted boiling water with a little vinegar.

For the Beurre Monte

- Whole butter cut into 3/8 inch cubes and chilled
- A saucepot with a thin layer of water - enough water to cover the bottom of the pan.

Preparation:

For the Lobster

1. Bring the lobster pot to a rolling boil.
2. Place lobsters in pot for approximately two minutes depending on the size of the lobster.
3. Remove the lobsters from the water and ice to cool just enough to handle.
4. The outer shells should be cooked enough to crack and slide the almost raw lobster meat out.
5. Place the shells aside and use for a lobster sauce or bisque.

For the Beurre Monte

1. Bring the water in the saucepot to a simmer.
2. Reduce heat to low and whisk in the butter one piece at a time to emulsify.
3. Keep heat very low and continue whisking to maintain emulsification.

Serving:

- Add lobster to the beurre monte and with the heat on low and gently cook the lobster until it tender. Do not boil or overcook or the lobster will lose flavor and texture. Think of it as cooking a steak medium rare.
- Your poached lobster can now be served plan in a warmed ramakin with crusty bread, over eggs benedict, pasta, rice, toast or used in lobster Newburg, lobster quiche or any other dish with lobster meat.

Riddle: How do you flatter a lobster?

Answer: You butter them up.

LOBSTER FUN QUIZ: TRUE OR FALSE

1. Lobster's have blue blood because it is high in copper.
2. Lobsters cannot grow back their legs or claws.
3. A young lobster sheds its shell around 25 times in their first five to seven years of life.
4. A lobster can live up to 50 years in the wild and weigh up to 45 pounds.
5. Lobster Reef is the name of a wine from Australia.
6. The North Atlantic lobster is the heaviest anthropoid in the world.
7. Larry the Lobster is both a real lobster and the largest lobster sculpture in New Zealand.
8. Homarus americanus is the scientific name for the North Atlantic lobster and has five pairs of legs and two large claws.
9. The Spanish artist Salvador Dali is well known for his creation of a lobster telephone.
10. During the Civil War in the United States in the 1860s, canned lobster was so inexpensive that it was used to feed soldiers.
11. The award-winning film 2016 film "The Lobster" starred Tom Cruise.
12. Miracle Whip Salad dressing cannot be called mayonnaise because it does not contain enough eggs.
13. Lobster Newburg was served in the 1920s on the New York Central Train system with New Wax Beans Fermiere, and Julienne Potatoes for $2.25.
14. Native Americans ate lobsters and used their shells for fertilizer to grow crops.
15. Lord Byron is quoted to have said "Europe's the mayonnaise, but America supplies the good old lobster."

QUIZ ANSWERS

1. True
2. False. Lobster often shed their legs and claws in fights or if they get trapped. They grow them back.
3. True
4. True
5. False. It is from New Zealand
6. True
7. True
8. True
9. True
10. True
11. False. It stared Colin Farrel
12. False. It does not have enough vegetable oil
13. True
14. False. It was D.H Lawrence

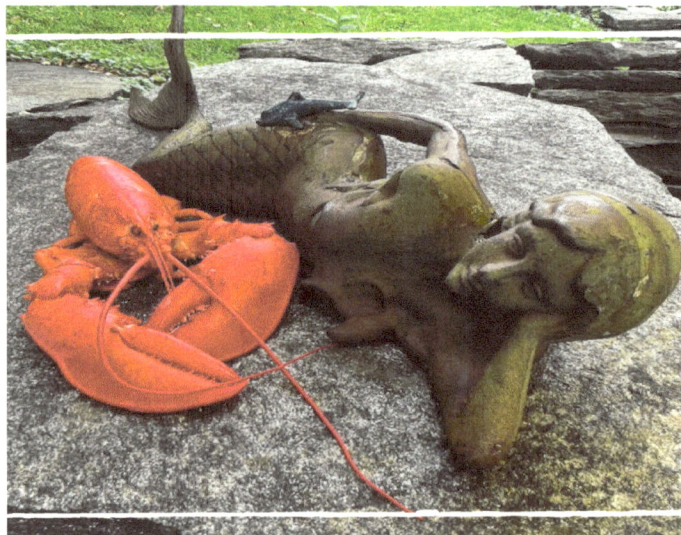

REFLECTIONS

Reflecting upon this collection of lobster recipes from around the world, I would like to pause a moment to remember that all cultures express gratitude for the food they eat. Many of these expressions of gratitude come in the form of prayer to a god, deity, or higher spirit. Others focus on nature, the earth, and the creatures with whom we share this planet that give their lives to give us sustenance. Whatever its form, recognizing we are one with and not above other living things on this planet is an important remembrance, responsibility, and practice. In closing I would like to share with you an often-spoken Native American blessing:

"We thank Great Spirit for the resources that made this food possible. We thank the Earth Mother for producing it, and we thank all those who labored to bring it to us. May the wholesomeness of the food before us, bring out the wholeness of the Spirit within us."

The Great Wave at Kanagawa

Milton Keynes UK
Ingram Content Group UK Ltd.
UKHW051610081224
452130UK00002B/12